Praise for Two Mirrors and a Cheetah

'A career's worth of learning and deep insights packaged for easy consumption. A must read for everyone who wants to build a career that brings out and develops the best of themselves.'
Jamie Heywood, Regional General Manager UK, Northern & Eastern Europe, Uber

'Engaging, entertaining and thought provoking. For anyone seeking to further their professional career and frankly for anyone seeking to unleash their true self in business or in life, this book is one not to miss!'
Leila McKenzie-Delis, Author, Founder and CEO, DIAL Global

'This book holds a career's worth of wisdom from an inspirational leader. I'm so pleased that Fiona has gone to the trouble of setting it down so honestly and clearly, I just wish I'd had the chance to read it much earlier in my career! Read this if you want a happier and healthier career!'
Doug Gurr, Director of the Natural History Museum and former CEO, Amazon UK

'Dedicated to exploring and understanding yourself, this book is packed with inspiring, insightful and practical advice and exercises to get you to where you want to go. The wisdom in these pages is priceless.'
Amanda Mackenzie OBE, Chief Executive, Business In the Community

'Engaging, authentic and easy-to-read, this book is like having your own personal career coach giving you the confidence and clarity to tackle anything. If your career has plateaued, or you're unhappy in your job but not sure what to do, then this book is essential reading.'
Ruwan Kodikara, VP Sony Music

'Fiona has created a narrative to help us all understand how we can thrive in our careers and how we can help others achieve their rhythm. I highly recommend this book not just for work, but for the universal truths found within it that will help you thrive in life too.'
Matthew Phelan, Author and Co-Founder, The Happiness Index.

'A highly engaging and valuable career guide, helpful at any stage in your career. McDonnell's path is a distinguished one, and through her unique lens, that of scientist, seasoned business leader, adventurous soul and life-long learner, she provides relatable, practical advice and frameworks that offer the reader a roadmap to growth and career satisfaction, a means to flourish professionally on one's own terms.'
Ripa Rashid, Author and Diversity and Inclusion Expert

TWO MIRRORS

AND A

CHEETAH

Think Differently,
Own Your Career &
Succeed by Being Yourself

FIONA McDONNELL

Published in the UK by Double Magpie

www.fionamcdonnell.com

Cover art by G Sharp Design, LLC
Interior layout and typesetting by waynekehoe.com

ISBN 978-1-7399263-0-4

FIRST EDITION 2021

Double Magpie Ltd
27 Old Gloucester Street,
London WC1N 3AX

www.doublemagpie.com

For Riemer, you embrace my 'crazy'.

*For Jasper and Elliot, you inspire me
more than you will ever know.*

Contents

PART 2
APPLYING THE KNOWLEDGE

Ten action steps to land your next job. Preparing your mind, materials and story. Creating opportunities, networking, being proactive and selective. Remaining true to yourself and learning throughout the process.

Considering alternatives to the full-time employment approach.

Ten tips for building an internal career path. Learning the process, identifying growth opportunities and maintaining choice. Getting involved in the organisation and bringing your supporters on board.

Transitioning successfully to the role of manager. Being a first-time manager or manager of peers.

Strategies for surviving an incompatible manager. Not blaming yourself, understanding the challenge, having open conversations, seeking neutral perspectives and moving on constructively.

Introduction

IF I ASKED YOU to describe yourself as a piece of pasta, to tell me the type of pasta you identify with the most and why you chose it, do you think you would have an answer? This is a question I asked three senior guest speakers whom I was introducing during an industry conference in 2006. It was the after-lunch session, otherwise known as the graveyard shift, and so I wanted to do something that was a little fun and would capture the audience's attention.

The speakers had little prior warning – I only let them know what I planned about 30 minutes before the start. Fortunately for me, not only did they oblige, but they entered into the challenge with amazing humour and energy. Each one of them was very quickly able to tell me not just which piece of pasta they chose but the fine detail as to why that shape was a good representation of who they think they are. It was not only entertaining; it was fascinating! We had rigatoni, chosen for its simple but powerful shape, cylinders being the strongest shape there is structurally. There was penne, similar in structure, reliability and strength to the rigatoni, but a little bit edgy as dictated by the slanting edge. I also volunteered the farfalle, a bow-shaped pasta; a romantic, artistic yet symmetrical shape which is delicate to look at though sharp edges become apparent when viewed up close.

Now, if I ask a room full of people to describe their unique skills or characteristics, I am frequently met with a long silence. There are even more blank stares and some uncomfortable shifting in seats, too, if I ask whether they are being 'themselves' at work, and whether they feel they are thriving.

I find this so fascinating. Most of us spend five out of seven days working, and a mere fraction of that time eating pasta. So, why the hesitation when the question is not abstract? Why do we not have the same handle on bigger things that matter as we do on what kind of pasta we would be? Imagine if you could describe with the same passion, precision and interest the straightforward, non-abstract things about you that are unique, as you can the kind of fruit you are or what animal best represents you. Imagine if you could just as easily talk about the things that excite you or the conditions that bring out your happiest or most productive self.

Perhaps we can even use that insight to break free from the expectations and filters that society dictates and be that person in practice. Maybe we could even follow the wisdom of the animal kingdom – like birds who fly south for the winter – and seek out environments that support us physically and mentally during our time at work? We are, after all, supposed to be the most intelligent species... and yet we put up with damaging contexts.

But, of course, it's not one or the other, abstract or concrete, is it? It's both. Abstract pictures let our creativity free and aid our understanding. These seemingly silly, metaphorical questions help us to talk about the not-silly truths of who we are and how we work. If we approach what is often presented as a rather serious topic in a different, more light-hearted way, we can access a greater understanding of ourselves. With patience and practice, it can all become second nature.

Mental images help us to relate to complicated topics. Abstract creativity helps us access understanding. Stories and anecdotes help us relate to and remember ideas. So, it follows that the right demonstration has the power to make tough topics fun; to not only land the message with your audience but enable them to actually commit it to memory.

Even 30 years after studying engineering at university, I can still recall complicated manufacturing concepts brought to life with storytelling in the book, *The Goal,* by Eliyahu Goldratt. Far from a theoretical textbook, it managed to enliven the topic by utilising narrative tools. In that same time, nothing in the field of softer skills or workplace psychology has landed as well for me as *The Goal* did in the field of engineering. I believe that it takes a lot of effort, and probably a lot of bravery, to be yourself at work, though it is a true source of power and advantage for those who succeed in doing so. I wanted to create something using visual metaphor and which had practical application to help people get a better grasp on what can be difficult topics to deal with, but which are so fundamental to equipping everyone to succeed just as they are.

The goal of *Two Mirrors and a Cheetah* is just that: to provide inspiration via an abstract idea, a metaphor or a mental image that will bring some simple and yet powerful career lessons to life. The key concept is based around a three-step framework, designed to challenge you to think differently and build a greater understanding of these key themes:

1. Knowing yourself – mirror one

2. Being yourself in reality – mirror two

3. Context and how it affects you – the cheetah

Together, these themes can help you take control of your career, navigate change and find greater fulfilment – through the magical method of just being yourself. Easier said than done, of course, but I am a firm believer that we are all more effective and happier when we do things as ourselves.

How to use this book

The book is broadly split into two parts. The first half is dedicated to developing an understanding and the second half to exploring how to apply the knowledge in different situations.

Part 1: Chapters 1 to 4 are about generating knowledge and introducing the mental pictures behind each of the mirrors and the cheetah to aid discovery and memory of the concepts. The different stories uncover the impact and development of self-awareness, self-belief, confidence and self-control: the ability to be oneself and filter feedback via the mirrors. This is followed by a detailed look at both the work conditions you require and the needs that must be met in order to succeed and feel fulfilled. Together, I refer to this as 'context', and it is the heart of the metaphor of the cheetah.

In each chapter I share the story of how the lesson behind the concept landed for me. I then seek, for each of these, not only to answer why it is important but also to suggest ways for you to increase your own understanding. I propose questions that challenge you to look at your career and situation with an objective eye. I also offer a few targeted, simple exercises that help you to be honest with yourself as a first step to evaluating your status quo.

Part 2: Chapters 5 to 11 will look at what you can do with this new understanding. These chapters address a range of career movements, both externally and internally, from the challenges of moving jobs to that of promotions, changing roles and managers, as well as how to leverage this framework to manage your own team.

Change, and how to adapt to it, is a thread that runs through the advice. Each section offers steps to guide you through these moments and to provide the encouragement for you to leverage what you learned in Part 1. We then close out the book with a look at how you can maintain these concepts in your life, encouraging you to model your newfound adaptability to help others and further aid the momentum towards a more diverse and inclusive world of work.

To bring the concepts in this book to life, I use examples from my own life and career, deconstructing them very openly to extract the learnings and weaving those through the story. Whether it's circumstances, choices or life events, much of our career path is down to chance, no matter how hard we attempt to plan it. So, the chances of my choices and situations matching up with any one of yours is slim. There is no 'right' route for a career, there is only *your* route. My hope is that the lessons within this book will be transferable to your situation, whatever industry, country or culture you live and work in; whether you are starting out on your career journey, developing yourself after a number of years in work or indeed facing the challenge of a big career change and transition. In all these cases, the following chapters can inspire you and guide you, both in your current role and your next move. I hope you enjoy reading.

PART 1

BUILDING UNDERSTANDING

1

Know Yourself – Mirror One

No CAREER journey is smooth, and mine certainly wasn't: it was a rollercoaster of running into walls, enjoying successes and learning from failures. When I look back across my career to date, reflecting on my many different challenges, there is no question that I have grown, shaped by those experiences, to become the person I am today. Among all of those experiences, there are a few key ones – some pivotal learning moments – that stand out for me. Strangely, the things which I found most difficult to learn were things I didn't even think I needed to focus on. Many of those moments, although I wasn't to know it at the time, turned out to be the start of big changes in my life and career. With reflection, I'm sure any of us could describe many such moments, both big and small, but for me, three key triggers stand out.

- **The leadership course**

About 10 or 15 years ago, I was on a training course for leaders. A mentor of mine was describing the most important moments or lessons in his own journey, and top of his list was gaining self-awareness. I can remember exactly how I reacted to that, and I distinctly remember thinking: 'Really? Ugh, this is just far too soft and touchy-feely! Just tell me what to actually *do.*' Despite the advice being laid out, plain and simple, I didn't want to hear it, and it was only later that I made the connection between this moment and another I had experienced earlier in my career.

• The performance review

In my early 30s, I was working for Nike in the first role where I actually had a profit and loss (P&L) responsibility and a team who reported to me. The role was a hybrid channel manager and part of the sales organisation. Up to that point I'd mainly had strategic projects or supporting roles, so there was lots to learn. In this role, I received a performance appraisal that was less 'shining' than I would have liked. As a self-proclaimed overachiever, although there was nothing actually *wrong* with this performance appraisal, I was unhappy because, up to that point, I had only ever been in the very top percentiles. My manager tried to explain to me why the appraisal was what it was and, perhaps more importantly, why I shouldn't just expect to be the best all the time. He said he didn't know what 'brand Fiona' stood for, and that I couldn't *create demand* for myself and my skills if I didn't know what I wanted to be known for delivering.

Now, the fact that I was taken down a peg or two, although unpleasant at the time, served to make me a lot more grounded as an individual. However, the real lesson came later for me – after the leadership course that I went on when I made the connection between them. Of course, what my old manager was trying to explain is that I lacked sufficient self-awareness to know who I was and what my brand at work was. Other than being some kind of ephemeral idea of 'the best', I didn't know what I wanted out of life, my career and my reputation. So, that's twice that self-awareness was brought to my attention.

- **The Christmas present**

The final, 'eureka' moment of insight for me was completely unconnected to the work world. There was a time in my life when many of my friends and family were starting to settle down, get married and have kids. I too had imagined I would be doing just that, but life (as it so often does) had not followed the naïve plans I had made as a young student. I was following my sense of adventure and pursuing a globetrotting career, but I was still single. One Christmas during this time, I received a present from one of my sisters: a book called *If I'm So Wonderful, Why Am I Still Single?* by Susan Page. In my family, we do have a habit of ribbing or teasing each other with sarcasm, but that was a bit of a boxing glove to the nose to be honest. Let's just say that the conversation wasn't exactly flowing over the turkey that Christmas! To be fair, she did have a point. As befits my pattern, the point was not one I wanted to hear at the time, so I put it on the shelf to collect dust and it wasn't until months later that I did eventually read the book.

So, altogether, these three moments made me stand still and ask myself: am I heading in the direction I want to? Do I know what my unique capabilities are and what I want to be or do? Am I communicating to the world what I want it to hear and see, and if not, then what should I do? It won't surprise you to hear that the answers to these questions were, of course, 'No'. Having steamed ahead in my life and career, moved around a lot, and done a lot of exciting things, some brave and some stupid, I had never questioned whether I was in control of where I was going.

The realisation that I was without a purpose or a plan, particularly for a structured and organised engineer like myself, was a really stark moment. Slowing down was not a phrase that was in my vocabulary, but it was a necessary step for me to take stock and, ultimately, to change or confirm the direction in which my life was heading.

> **Reflection – Eureka moments**
> Can you think of any pivotal experiences that had a profound impact on you in the way my trigger moments did on me? What were they? Is there a common theme?

Look in the mirror and take in your reflection; no filters. Are you happy with what you see, looking beyond the physical? It takes a lot of honesty to consider this.

The mirror one metaphor is all about understanding everything that is you: what is working and what is not. In short, it's all about the many layers of self-awareness that are possible – not just the simple awareness that took me on a leadership course, but the deeper awareness that meant I had to listen to advice I didn't want to hear and make changes in response. It is about getting comfortable with who you actually are and understanding what you're good at as well as what you are not so good at. It's about looking in the mirror and being honest with yourself about what your values and priorities are and where your passions lie. Look deeply into this metaphorical mirror to know how you are perceived and how you impact others. It's about taking time to reflect in order to choose what to accept about yourself and what to set out to change.

Why does self-awareness matter?

You can motor through life without giving it a second thought, as a great deal of people do. I am guessing, however, given you picked up this book, that you know that there are multiple benefits to be had by getting to know yourself a lot better. Here are just some of the reasons that a bit more self-awareness makes sense.

Authenticity

Personally, I think real self-awareness is very much aligned with the concept of authentic leadership (if you will excuse a somewhat over-used buzz phrase). Essentially, if you are always busy trying to be somebody else, then when times get tough, it's going to be hard to keep this up. If you're already being yourself, and not expending energy on a façade or an act, then you are, in many ways, walking the path of least resistance. It's not something that will change or require sustaining as your circumstances evolve.

However, authenticity is a difficult thing to achieve right out of the starting blocks, largely because we are surrounded by examples that we copy to some extent. We are often inspired by people and aim to work like those we respect; at least, that's how I started my career. Without thinking about it, we observe how various people do and don't behave, and naturally we want to be like those we like best; often those who look successful or popular.

This is something which goes back to how we were as kids in the playground. I see that lesson quite acutely with my two boys: as they are learning who they are and how to be, they are very easily influenced by TV characters or other schoolchildren and they frequently copy what they see. As we start out in life, role models can stoke our ambition, particularly if there is something to aim for, like perfecting a skill or achieving something.

This isn't necessarily a bad thing. Two people who I admire and aspire to emulate in my work are Sir John Harvey-Jones, former ICI board chairman and an original troubleshooter, whose ability to look with the eyes of an outsider helps to solve problems, and entrepreneur Richard Branson, whose fearlessness to take his brand to adjacent markets inspires me. The difference is, though, that while I aspire to have the same type of impact as these people, I go about it in a very different way. This is necessary as my personality is likely to be far from that of Sir John Harvey-Jones or Richard Branson. I need to understand what *my* way is going to be. If I try to do the same things as them in the same way, I will only ever be a poor copy of these people.

The longer we work, the more important it is to have our *own* identity and to be happier with who *we* are. By all means, be inspired by other individuals, but pick up bits and pieces from them that you can adapt for your own style. Don't try to replicate others. Self-awareness will help you to discern what your own style is so that you don't have to emulate someone else.

Managing your energy

If you try to work in a way that needs skills that don't fit you and leaves skills that you're good at unused, then arguably it's going to take a lot more energy for you to achieve things. On the other hand, recall the feeling of time flying by as you hit your groove and get in the zone. When you're good at or passionate about something, it usually takes a lot less energy. I find that when I'm really enjoying something and getting a great deal out of it, I can finish the task, performance or exercise with more energy than when I started. When I have more energy, I have better focus, so naturally my results are better and I have more impact.

There are many ways to develop your self-awareness around the things and people that give you energy, and those that drain you of that energy. For me, it was early motherhood. Like many new mothers, I was so tired and had so much to achieve with so little energy, that I soon began to notice where I naturally got energy from and what naturally took energy away from me. This meant, for me, learning that some people absolutely ruined my day and that saying 'no' to them on occasion was going to be required. Then, there were some activities that appeared to require energy, like sport, but which gave me energy back when I made time for them.

Remember that what energises you will not necessarily be the same things that energise others. Try and observe what activities feel like and you will be able to identify those ones that work for you. Understanding these little details can give you a huge ability to shape your situation for the better.

Good mental health

Anxiety and mental health challenges are common, yet we don't talk enough about them as a society. If you have ever received any kind of coaching, therapy or treatment for mental health issues, you will know that self-awareness is a key part of maintaining good mental wellbeing, and in fact, a lack of self-awareness can lead to strain. Being able to drop things or not take things to heart, or simply cut through the chaos of work and life, is far easier when you know a lot about yourself and what drives you. Ignoring – or not being able to see – the signs in yourself of frustration, burnout or too high a level of stress, can lead to both physical illness and mental health problems. When I first had a panic attack – something that research suggests is experienced by around 12% of people[1] – I didn't know what it was. I let things continue unchecked and experienced two more, followed by acute agoraphobia that meant I could not leave my apartment easily. I sought advice from a counsellor who helped me identify the built up 'baggage' in my life that was responsible. Honesty, letting go of the past plus a gradual step outside every day, got me back out there. Now that I am aware of my mental fitness and have built a habit of regularly checking in with myself, things don't build and I haven't had any more attacks. With my self-awareness now somehow automatic, I prioritise mental health alongside my physical health.

You may be fortunate enough to never need formal intervention or medication for your mental health (although something like as many as one in four of us will at some point in our lives[2]), but mental wellbeing is just as important as physical. Just as you might be aware of a sudden twinge in your knee, a new mole that wasn't there before or a headache that won't go away, self-awareness is key for maintaining good mental health.

The job hunt and your CV

Trying to write a compelling CV or resume will be extremely difficult if you aren't sure what you are offering. As technology makes connecting with people and companies so infinitely possible, and job applications per advertised job increase, being able to represent your added value and rise above the rest is becoming a fundamental step in getting recognised.

No one buys a product if they can't find out from the packaging what it is and what it offers, and job hunting is no different; your CV is part of your packaging, and it needs to sell you before you even get in the room.

Then, later in the process, you have the interview, where you can expect to be asked about yourself from many angles, including those not covered in your CV. Self-awareness will be key to providing engaging answers here too. We will get into more detail about this specific topic later in the book.

People impact

Like it or not, each of us shares this world with other people, and the way we interact affects everyone. Understanding the impact we have on others is a very important part of self-awareness. There are different employment set-ups, different working relationships, different types of people and different characters, so this is a complex and nuanced area.

Throughout your education, you are competing, for the most part, against yourself and 'the system'. Your exam results are a result of your work; it's not really a collaborative effort. However, almost without exception, when you enter the work world, you will be working with people and achieving things together, whether you're a manager or a team player. The reality is that the dynamics of teams, how you work with people and how people can access and work with you, are central to achieving results – and it's not something that we, as a society, teach our children. It's an area that I have worked hard on for myself, as it was definitely a blind spot for a while – perhaps you've had a similar experience. I derived much of my confidence from my academic track record, and I didn't immediately realise how important it is to value the contributions of others. As an ambitious individual and an extrovert, I was also at risk of not sharing or diverting the limelight frequently enough. As I matured as a manager, I learnt how people perceived me, and fortunately, over the years, I have been able to adapt. Sharing and caring more for others, and understanding and meeting my own recognition or self-esteem needs in different ways, has made me a more balanced person, while preserving my ambition, and self-awareness is a key component of this.

Leadership

If you are, or aspire to be, a leader, you'll probably know that your every move can be scrutinised when you're in a position of leadership. A lack of self-awareness leads to blind spots about the ways in which you struggle and succeed, which, particularly for a leader under the microscope, can in turn lead to the kind of scrutiny that can bring you down. Being aware of your capabilities and emotions, especially your stressors, will allow you to better control yourself and to work more effectively. In doing so, you can make clearer and better decisions. Lack of self-awareness can cloud your judgement and eventually lead people to doubt you, which will weaken your ability to motivate, inspire and to lead purposefully. If you want to inspire people, I would argue that self-awareness is a fundamental requirement.

How do you improve your self-awareness?

There are many levels to understanding yourself beyond the strict definition of self-awareness. The context for this book is career navigation and so the relevant elements of self-awareness include: strengths, skills, weaknesses or development areas, passions, values, goals, characteristics of your personality and preferences for how you work. Also included is a mix of the emotions and desires that drive your behaviour, how you interact with others in different situations and, as a result of the above, how others view you.

To capture or uncover all these elements together, it is sometimes easier to create a picture in your mind. Imagine you were to describe yourself as a packaged product; if you could design your packaging in a way that communicates you and all that you have to offer, including your ingredients list and instructions for use and handling. What would it say? Perhaps packaged products are not your thing. Then how about Top Trumps or a Pokémon card or even a car manual; what would it contain that represents you? It doesn't matter what sort of picture or structured format you choose. The point is that, by doing so, you start to see how many different dimensions you have. You understand how these are all useful seen together, to give an accurate description of you, what you have to offer, how you like to work and how you want to be treated. It prompts you to think about how you are going to communicate with the outside world. The list of creative possibilities is endless, but what is important is that it is something that works for you. That it helps you explore and capture all your dimensions, from your superpowers to your nemeses.

So, now we have clarified what self-awareness is and why it is important, how do you go about getting more of it? Well, deciding that you want to be more self-aware is already a good first step. For some, the process can be a long, soul-searching journey – but it doesn't have to be. When I eventually got my head around the idea of improving my own self-awareness, I had visions of spiritual retreats and countless hours spent meditating or thinking about the meaning of life. These images spring to mind when people first introduce the idea of touchy-feely soft skills and topics that are essentially personal. But, if that feels off-putting or daunting to you, don't worry. Rest assured, the ideas and tools in this book are simple and can be used by anyone, anytime. Although they require you to be honest and reflective, they are practical and full of common sense. And it's not going to take up all of your time either – so don't worry about having to quit the day job just to learn more about yourself!

As we focus on careers, let's split self-awareness into the following four areas which collectively make what we'll call your **product map**. Effectively, this is a way of presenting what you bring to any work situation. The four parts of your product map are:

- Your **toolkit**. Your capabilities and strengths, your weaknesses or development needs, your personality and your experience and knowledge.

- Your **motivators**. Your values, passions, where you get your energy, what drives you, the ambitions or goals you have and the priorities you form.

- Your preferred **work style**. This includes behavioural traits, your character, types of work culture and your role within a team.

- Your **impact** on others and how you are perceived. This translates to your reputation and what 'pushes your buttons' – the pressure points and how you react.

Let's now explore a couple of different options for developing your own knowledge of these parts of yourself. This process will be about finding what you are comfortable with and what works for you. It goes without saying that, unless you are committed to gaining insight about yourself and are willing to be honest in the process, then the results will not be impactful – so don't feel tempted to fudge your answers! Give it a go.

Step 1: Start by assessing the size of the challenge

Making an inventory of where you are at now is important, even if only to reflect on how much you already know about yourself. The aim of this step is to be conscious and accepting of the grey areas or missing pieces. It really is a strength to know what you don't know.

Depending on where you are in your career, it might surprise you to see how far you've come without questioning these things before. However, try not to get distracted by second guessing past decisions at this stage. We can reflect on these at a later stage if it's helpful. Right now, we're just making an inventory. Take the four elements of self-awareness (toolkit, motivators, work style, impact) to start building your product map. See if you can write down exactly what those things are for you. You can use a notes app or a pen and paper. Alternatively, if you'd prefer a template, here's one to get you started.

FIGURE 1.1: YOUR PRODUCT MAP

Toolkit	Motivators	Work Style	Impact
Skills / Strengths	Passions	Behavioural Default	Reputation
Development (Weaknesses)	Values	Character	Perception of Colleagues
Personality	Energy	Team Roles	Perception of Manager
Experience / Knowledge	Ambitions / Goals*	Working Culture	Red Buttons (Stressers)

*Goals are not strictly something that relate to self-awareness, though an ambition or dream might give you insight into what your priorities are. A goal is more specific; it is something you decide and set. If you already have some, that's great, and you should include them here anyway. If you don't have an 'ambition' or 'dream' to include, we will address how to develop goals at the end of this chapter.

You may be able to write pages of notes on this with very little prompting. If so, great! But don't panic if not. This is a difficult exercise for many people – even *most* people, I'd say – so here is some structure and guidance to help you think about your answers in more depth.

Your toolkit

Let's start with the first column. What is a skill, and what is a strength? Think of the things you can do, then think of the things that you do *really well*. Being able to do it is a skill or capability; it's often one you have had to acquire. A skill becomes a strength when you are better at it than other things you can do, or better at it than other people. Examples of skills employers look for could be an ability to work well in teams, organisation, problem solving, selling, creativity, using software like Excel, programming or coding, technical skills, people skills, communication, leadership and time management. Often, when something you can do is also something you *like* doing, this makes you better at it, and it becomes a strength more easily.

Once you have your list of skills, ask yourself what you are good at relative to other people. This way, you build your relevant strengths for employers who look at you in comparison to other candidates. Take PowerPoint, for example. If you can work fluently with this software then it would be a skill. However, if you deliver compelling presentations, the best in class, then this might be more of a strength for you. Or, think about driving a lorry. It is not something we are born to do, so it takes learning, and thus it is a skill that you acquire. But it is a basic requirement for all lorry drivers and therefore not a strength compared to others. However, you may be able to reverse into the tightest spot, or do a three-point turn on a tiny coin! This would be a strength when compared to other drivers. The emphasis here is on your ability relative to most people in your area of work. What is it that you are strongest doing and what makes you stand out?

I asked my husband to do this exercise. He put sailing in, as he enjoys it and felt he was good at it. Eventually though, he took it out, thinking it wasn't relevant to his work in house renovations. Given he used to deliver boats and can reverse park them in strong winds, I would certainly call that a strength! I see why he decided to leave it out, but I think he limited himself by doing so. Don't make the same mistake; choose the things you are strong at regardless of where you use them to start with. Otherwise you are creating a biased and blinkered view. The idea is to choose work that uses what you can do and incorporates what you like all in one – not to let the parameters of your current work dictate what you can be good at!

When it comes to weaknesses, try putting it in a more constructive way. What are you developing, or working to improve? Take a tennis player who has the skill of playing tennis. She has a power serve and a less powerful backhand. Working to improve the least strong item (her weakness) is the area of development.

Moving on from there, how would you describe your personality? Are you outgoing or shy? Laid back or focused and determined? Hopefully those questions can provide a starting point to help you understand your unique toolkit. Other people can often describe your personality better than you can off the top of your head, so ask a couple of people close to you if you are unsure. It can help to think in terms of adjectives: friendly, creative, structured, energetic, lazy, imaginative, sociable etc.

Your motivators

Think of the things that drive you. In a career context, many people put passions – or what they like and enjoy – to one side. It's considered unimportant or somehow unprofessional, but I don't think these things are irrelevant at all. What you are passionate about is all part of the inventory of 'you', and a key component of self-awareness. Asking whether you know what you're passionate about might sound like a strange question, but I've found that very few of us start out life knowing what we are put on this earth to do. I'm very envious of people who know, right from the beginning, what their purpose is. For the rest of us mere mortals, discovering what we are truly passionate about takes time. Start by thinking about the things you have done where time flies by, a clear sign that you're enjoying yourself. Or perhaps things that you look forward to rather than dread. What are those activities?

Next, perhaps you have strong values that shape what you do and where you place importance? Don't just think about the obvious must-haves, but also what you consider to be unacceptable things or no-go areas. This is often an effective way to uncover your core values. Honesty, integrity and fairness are core for me, for example, and I arrived at this conclusion from knowing how much I can't bear dishonesty, lack of integrity and unfairness. Values are key to being 'you', so think about what you stand for or where you will draw the line and on what issues you have strong opinions.

In addition to passions and values, have you thought about your ambitions or big picture goals? Do you have a life mission? Are you aiming for something specific, or do you just wish to enjoy every day? Have you thought about what you want to achieve in the job you're doing right now? Don't worry about forming goals from scratch; simply recognise the ones that exist for you at this stage and put them in your inventory. Leave it blank if it's a question you haven't yet answered for yourself.

The same applies to where you get your energy and how you set your priorities – the things that are immediately important to you. For the latter, think of things like your family, health, sport, time alone, socializing and walking the dog.

Again, many people don't think about this until they're forced to make trade-offs as circumstances change. But, maybe you do know this about yourself already. What energises you? It could be types of people, situations or activities. Think of those moments when you find yourself with a spring in your step or a feeling that you can conquer the world. What made you feel that way? Perhaps try and identify what gave you energy and what eroded it over the last seven days? Is there a connection? Perhaps it is working on things that you like or simply getting your list of tasks done. Observing these feelings more will yield the insight you need.

Your work style

If the toolkit is the *'what'* and the motivators the *'why'*, then style is the *'how'*. Look at interactions you have with colleagues, your manager and any team you are part of. Do you have a preferred work style? Leading, taking instructions, following tight work-flows, creating – these are just a few of the different working styles that there are. To identify these, ask yourself: do you like detailed instructions or loose direction? Do you fear or get excited by a blank page? Do you thrive on or avoid responsibility? Are you chaotic or deeply systematic? How do you communicate or deal with conflict? We all have a 'default' work style classed as one of four formal types: logical, detailed oriented, supportive and idea oriented. If you know yours, make a note. Do you know what organisational cultures you would best fit in? Formal, informal, team oriented? What specific team roles would work best for you? Co-ordinator, supporter, idea generator, coach? When understanding your character, you may need others to help you see what traits you have. Often confused with personality, character is conditioned or learned behaviours that build over time, whereas personality is in-built. Imagine you are going to a dance. If personality is the shoes you wear, then character is the place you choose to dance or the way you dance; it comes from within. There are positive and negative traits in all of us and identifying both shows real understanding of who you are. Think about things like sincerity, integrity, grit, tolerance and courage on the plus side and abrasiveness, dominance or deceitfulness on the negative side.

Impact

Finally, are you aware of how people view you and what perceptions you create? Do know what you have a reputation for? Do you have sufficient feedback and knowledge from colleagues and close associates about how your interactions shape them? You can either ask people in order to get the insight, or failing that, try putting yourself in others' shoes. What would your best friend say about you? What would a teammate or manager say? Try and get a range of feedback captured through different people's eyes. Understanding how people perceive you and how your behaviour affects them is a difficult thing to think about on your own, so don't worry if you find this challenging. Even considering the question a little will boost your awareness. Finally, as you consider interactions with colleagues and how you feel in certain conditions, can you see what pushes your buttons and what your stressors are? Again, at this stage the answers don't matter. What is important is asking yourself the question and making that inventory.

If you've just gone through that exercise, you will likely either have lots of blanks or, alternatively, you will have lists that are far too long to be specific. If you have lots of blanks, and an absence of information, then you are missing the opportunity to shine a light on what makes you great. This means the unique power you have is likely to be going to waste. If, on the other hand, you had very long lists, then there is equally a high chance that the genuinely unique elements are going underutilized in favour of something in the list that is less 'you'. Are you able to do something with that insight? Just imagine what this means for you in terms of utilising what you bring. How do you shape your leadership style and how are you selling yourself through your CV? This even shapes how you run your weekly schedule. Let's look at how to change that in Step 2.

Step 2: Trial multiple approaches to drive further understanding

There are many ways to begin filling in the blanks or narrowing down your thoughts, as needed. As we know, this is not a one-size-fits-all approach. Take what you need from the following tools and techniques to help you build out your product map.

The structured self-assessment

This is particularly good for understanding your toolkit and motivators, especially where these may not be immediately evident. There are lots of books and models out there that will guide you through a more formal and in-depth self-assessment of your strengths and motivators. Depending on the specific book you choose, expect to look at things systematically and with depth and patience but not always in ways that are immediately apparent. The book, *What Color is Your Parachute,* by Richard N Bolles, is just one example of a framework and a seemingly timeless text. First published in around 1970, it is frequently updated and generations of people have found it useful. I have gone through the processes in this book a number of times myself, with changing outcomes on each occasion as I have grown throughout my life. It contains simple exercises for capturing insights about yourself without being overly directive.

I would recommend this structured option for people who want a more formulaic approach to get started. The structure forces you to not only think of a range of things that could be the answers you need, but to be focused and precise about those things that are at the heart of who you are. It doesn't necessarily have to be a career or self-help book you seek out. There are similar approaches in many books on personal branding. *Personal Branding for Dummies,* by Susan Chritton, or *Brand You,* by John Purkiss and David Royston-Lee, are two alternatives that explore your skill set. Basically, these books and models all require you to question what it is that you have and what you value, in order to better market and communicate yourself to the world.

Whichever process you follow, you may find that you end up with results with which you disagree – but this is actually a good thing! It is the thought process of introspection and evaluation that is most important. If an exercise tells you that you have a particular strength in organising things or being creative, but you think you are the most disorganised person, without a creative bone in your body, then consider the facts. What has led you to this conclusion that the method didn't look for? Or, perhaps you need to shift your outlook. It might be that you work in a job that has never required you to demonstrate these skills, so you don't recognise them? Maybe they're not top of mind because you haven't used them in a while?

In my case, I was initially looking for skills that I was using in my day job, which put a really narrow lens on my view. It was only when I took a look at the wider scope of my activities that I saw skills I had that were equally valuable. For example, although I never associated joy with planning or organising, I had enjoyed planning many social events. I was reluctant to include it and didn't really see it initially as anything other than administrative and (wrongly) thought the exercises would spit out a recommendation that I should work in a supportive, administrative role. As valuable and important as administrative services are, I envisaged myself in a totally different role. However, these methods showed me that planning is undeniably a skill I have. Following the process openly, instead of forming preconceived notions of what would happen, helped me look beyond the administrative element of planning to how crucial it is for strategy and leadership.

Creativity, too, was something I had always, again wrongly, associated exclusively with the arts. With the exception of a cartoon cat, which has taken years of practice, I can't really draw anything recognisable. However, I didn't think of creativity in a more expansive way, as a different way of presenting things, or as doing something entirely new, which is something I can do. I spent many years inadvertently mislabelling my skills or ignoring the skills I had, rather than exploring their potential and how best to use them. Structured approaches are great tools to help you open your eyes, expand your view of yourself, and focus in on what really makes you 'you'.

Formal assessments and diagnostics

Not a world away from the self-assessment approach, but far more detailed and specialised, are personality diagnostics or self-perception inventories, as they are sometimes called. These offer more tangential and sometimes abstract approaches that help you learn more about yourself and your default styles. In particular, they uncover the elements that are least obvious or subconscious. I have participated in multiple different programmes across my career, some individual, some team based, and there are new ones popping up all the time. From insight into your working mode and your preference for certain conditions, to your default role working within a team or your reaction working under pressure, there is a diagnostic out there for everything. Whether the characteristics you have are visible or hidden, if they affect how you perform, then there's merit in understanding them.

A quick Google search of personality tests will give you a

plethora of options. The theory essentially boils down to identifying and understanding five personality traits: extraversion, agreeableness, openness, conscientiousness and neuroticism. They look at how you perceive the world and how you make decisions, and some explore how you react under pressure. The Myers-Briggs Type Indicator (MBTI), is a very common one that has been around for 40 years and is very effective as a personal diagnostic. After answering a long list of questions, you are categorised into one of 16 set personality types. Free versions can give you a taster. There are plenty of comparisons of the typical characteristics that go hand in hand with the 16 types, plus suggestions of jobs that would suit each one. Other sources of personality tests include Insights Discovery or the nine Belbin Team Roles.

If you are a novice to this type of personal inventory, they are mostly questionnaire based, most of which require you to use instinct and make trade-offs and choices in seemingly unrelated contexts, sometimes under time constraints. They will then present you with what this means according to that particular test. There are no right or wrong answers, and you cannot pass or fail. It's also not something that is prescriptive or should limit how you understand yourself. In almost all cases, I found that the results did feel like 'me', but it's important to note that they are only a guide. The results helped me be more honest about my view of myself, as I had certain characteristics that were hidden, and they were not things I would have pulled out if asked in a more direct fashion. As long as you don't take them as gospel, or use them as an excuse, these kinds of diagnostics can be really interesting and a helpful way to start thinking about your self-awareness more deeply.

As the shape of work changes for so many people, with portfolio careers, the increase of the gig economy and with interim work more common than ever, many people are not going to have access to these more formal investment-style diagnostics through their workplaces. If you can, take a look at the free versions for a taster before forking out yourself on what can sometimes be pricey courses, in case it is not your thing. But, if it is useful, then I recommend making the investment. Interpreting the diagnostics in some of the leadership-based tests is often a skill in need of an expert; someone trained in the concept. Also, if you do take these types of tests, remember that they reflect you *at that time*. As we evolve and mature, expect the results to change. These tools are great at exploring team dynamics too, so will perhaps be helpful to you as you go on to lead. Further information on structured self-assessments and diagnostics is provided in the section on additional resources at the end of the book.

Learn by making 'mistakes'

Some people just like to get stuck in, throw caution to the wind and simply work in 'trial and error' mode. There is, after all, no such thing as a mistake in a career, just a suboptimal decision and a subsequent insight you didn't yet have. If that sounds like you, then making mistakes and correcting as you go could be a strong way of learning for you. This is often advice I give to younger people starting out in their career, those with a greater appetite for risk and perhaps less to lose if things do go wrong: simply try lots of things! Until you try something, it's not always obvious that you won't like it, or that you will enjoy it, or even be good at it. There is no wasted experience early in your career; you just build a different view. It's great for discovering passions and cultures that fit, or even strengths. Arguably, some of the biggest lessons are to be gained when making moves that turn out not to be quite right and using the pain of those situations to really understand what you don't like.

If you've ever done any speed dating, you'll understand what I mean here. I did in-person speed dating a number of times, a little before online dating had some real momentum, although I did do some of that too. I remember sitting for three minutes in front of individuals, trying to find something to say before the bell rang. In case you are wondering, three minutes is definitely not enough time to know if you really like somebody and are therefore destined to be with them for the rest of your life. However, three minutes can be an excruciatingly long time to try and talk to some of the characters I met, and a long time to try and talk to somebody that's obviously not right. It is also certainly long enough to decide that you don't want to see somebody again!

My career path worked in a similar way. Early on, I moved around a lot. I bounced, with some sort of logic, from one job to the other, with an average stay of about two years. Looking back, 20-30 years later, I think it was perfectly valid that I moved around and tried things, as I discovered more about my capabilities, and indeed, where those met with employers' needs. However, each time I moved, it was because I had run into something I either didn't like or wasn't patient enough to wait for. Perhaps I hadn't yet learnt the value of development conversations, networking or seeking out and landing the next opportunity internally. I simply took off, fuelled by my young, ambitious and stubborn self, to find it elsewhere. However, these lessons came later, after I was already much clearer on what I liked and didn't, as well as what I had to offer.

In a recent career development session, I was asked how I would explain moving around a lot in my career and how I would justify those choices. 'Job-hopping' is often seen as a red flag by recruiters and employers, and although I would not describe multiple-years stays as job-hopping exactly, some people did look askance at my work history at the time. My answer to this individual was this: that your CV or resume, your work history, this is your story. How you decide to tell it, and the reasons behind those moves you made, can make it either a bad story or a very credible story. Here's an example of how framing can change something from a flop into a learning experience. I made one move that was, in hindsight, completely wrong for me. The job description ticked all the boxes, but it fell short in reality. The lack of interaction with people, combined with it being a B2B (business to business) service rather than a consumer product, just didn't give me energy. I hadn't realised these were such strong needs of mine. However, instead of shamefully trying to gloss over this 'bad move' on my part, I now talk openly with recruiters about it, showing what I have learnt about myself and the clarity it gives me in knowing what I am looking for now.

Here's where the risk is: when you don't attempt to understand or describe the moves you have made, you leave recruiters and prospective employers to draw their own conclusions. Without first-hand knowledge of you, they are just as likely to fill in those gaps with negative explanations, so it's important to take control of your own story. Assuming you can do that, go ahead and try things, learning about yourself as you go!

Listen to your internal compass

We all have an internal compass, something that nudges us in a certain direction. The challenge for us is learning to hear it, listen to it and trust it. Sometimes you just know when something feels right or wrong, but many other situations are a bit more nuanced. This approach essentially means learning to listen to your gut, your heart, or your instincts, whatever you want to call it, and knowing when to go with that. It might sound a bit too wishy-washy, but it's just about recognising when something doesn't feel right. The more you do something driven by gut feel, the stronger your gut feel will become. Admittedly, developing your gut feel tends to come with years of experience, so this might be something suitable for a later career development or in conjunction with something a bit more consciously thought through, but let's not ignore the fact that instinct is an important and valuable way of gathering information about yourself and using it to make decisions.

Let me give you an example here. I have always followed my sense of adventure and my desire to attempt the seemingly impossible; I am also guided by my need for fairness. How do I know those things about myself? They are all things I can *feel*. The first two stir excitement, and that gives me energy, and the latter is a real source of irritation when it is not in abundance. I was offered a role in Warsaw, Poland, on my return from my first maternity leave, when my son was still only four months old. It was a country I hadn't visited, a language I didn't speak and the major upheaval of a relocation. Did I feel apprehension and risk while I considered it? No, I was on fire thinking of the adventure of such an opportunity! My internal compass brought my passions and desires to the fore such that I could see past the description on paper.

> **Reflection – Gut feelings**
> Can you recall decisions you have made where you could strongly *feel* your reaction like mine? Were they positive feelings or maybe waves of dread? What does this tell you about yourself?

Whether you follow your instinct boldly, or simply use it as a prompt to look at something more carefully, my advice is to notice when you have those moments of unwavering clarity driven by your own gut feel. Recognise *why* you think or feel like that, and look for what this means for you going forward. Perhaps it is because you are touching on a core value, or perhaps it's hitting a personal sore spot for you. Either way – instinct should not be ignored.

Seek Feedback

Input from other people is fundamental to getting a balanced picture of who you are. I believe that feedback is a gift and should be received gratefully. If you are to improve as you go through your career, it has a role to play in helping you to increase what you know about yourself. Feedback is widely used in businesses for the purpose of improving a product or service, so there's no reason why this shouldn't apply to you as an individual. The challenge lies in deciding what type of feedback to get, from whom to seek feedback and both the frequency and way in which you want to receive and digest the feedback.

Not everybody is able to give feedback in a way that is useful. In fact, many people can give feedback that can be unhelpful or, at worst, quite damaging. So, take a moment to reflect on whose feedback you would value. Who you ask is closely connected to *how* and *when* to ask for feedback. If you are looking to get an inventory of where you are at, then the annual review or the 360-degree feedback mechanisms are great for collecting a wider range of views. These are static, of course, and will need repeating over time. It is useful to seek feedback from multiple stakeholders beyond your manager who, of course, is a critical voice. Try to include team members, peers, customers and internal customers. Include direct reports too, if you are a manager, or the juniors around you. The key is that you don't only seek feedback from people who will tell you what you want to hear, but from enough parties who represent the spectrum of voices. This way, you keep yourself open to hearing different perspectives.

Remember, when talking about feedback, that you will get input and opinions on your actual skills and capabilities as well as on people's perceptions of your skills and capabilities. It is important to differentiate between the two and use this to decide on any action you choose to take. Given we are focusing on increasing self-awareness, the ideal outcome or situation would be one where your own view of your toolkit and work style is closely aligned to how others perceive them. This is difficult to achieve, and leaders work on it for years. So, if you are coming close to matching views, that's awesome: you are nailing self-awareness!

When working on performance and specific improvements, regular, in-the-moment feedback will be useful, with input from a few chosen feedback providers. Keeping it simple, you can ask for feedback on what you are doing well and what you are not doing so well. When asking for the developmental feedback, pose the questions in a way that help the person give you an example. You should also ask for advice on how you could change or improve, or suggestions for which elements or focus areas would benefit from improvement. Phrasing things in such a way will help to make sure all your feedback is constructive and that you can do something with it.

One more recent development is the use of employee engagement tools to gather feedback. This can be a particularly good tool for managers and leaders. From one-off annual surveys to frequent, sometimes daily, employee check-ins, this gives us huge insight into the sentiments of teams on a variety of topics, including how you are performing as a team lead or manager.

I used it to see where there were imbalances in expectations of me as a leader, with some liking autonomy and some more direction. Using this data, I was able to adjust my approach on an individual level. I was also able to see when morale slipped, even slightly, and was able to take action to steer us back on track. The collection of such frequent engagement data seemed extreme to me at first. Yet, having seen first hand the power this gives an organisation to benchmark across countries and businesses, and more importantly, to hold managers and the business units to account while protecting individual anonymity, I've been won over.

But, what about the *quality* of the feedback you are gathering?

We have probably all had a piece of feedback in our lives that was demotivating and ultimately useless, and mostly because of how it was phrased. Where is the value in telling somebody, 'I didn't like your report'? Or, 'You did a really bad job at stacking the pallets'? What is needed is to understand *why* the report wasn't liked or *why* the stacking was bad, and more importantly, what could have been done to improve next time.

You can't control how people will deliver their messages, of course, so the key for you will be learning to discern between unhelpful, untrue feedback, or feedback which is unhelpfully phrased but nevertheless contains useful information for you. Here's an example: I once received some particularly gendered feedback in a mid-year review. I was performing well versus my male colleagues, yet I was told I was 'too ambitious' and 'too focused on delivering'. Phrases like 'aggressive' and 'unlikeable if I were a man' were used, which smacked of sexism. It was therefore hard to accept it as objective and useful feedback. However, when I look back at that review and the conversations I had with my manager at the time, I now know that there could have been useful nuggets in there somewhere. Helping me decode what 'too ambitious' meant (assuming that it meant something valuable other than just 'Don't be a woman and ambitious'), would have been a transformative experience and potentially really useful to me. I was definitely overstretched, having taken on far too much, and real feedback on what to change would have been appreciated, but we didn't get there because the critical, sexist and unhelpful part was drowning it out. Without examples or context to help me see the issues more clearly, it wasn't useful.

Preparing to get feedback and learning to accept it regularly takes some getting used to. My advice would be to practise getting feedback in different ways, and also to practise giving it. The more you get used to it, the more you will learn to not take it personally but to treat it as the useful information source it is.

Also, remember that, ultimately, the power of what to *do* with that feedback always lies in your hands.

> **Reflection – Feedback channels**
> Do you have established avenues for feedback? Can you see which sources you could be missing? Any topic blind spots?

Get a mentor, be a mentor

Not to be confused with the role of manager, a mentor is somebody removed from your direct line reporting relationships and potentially somebody who you aspire to be like, somebody who inspires you and somebody who can connect you to opportunities or individuals that could help you progress in your career. I always advise people to choose and reach out to a mentor with those points in mind as opposed to being allocated a mentor. This is because the relationship the two of you build is fundamental to getting the best out of it.

Having a mentor, at its best, provides you with a neutral sounding board. I found having a mentor was a brilliant way of hearing the things that I didn't want to hear, some of them fundamental and harsh truths but always necessary. I am truly grateful to the mentors that I have had over the years.

Taking the chance to be a mentor, too, is not only a rewarding process but a chance for learning in and of itself. Helping somebody else to reflect and see how they can approach the challenges they face opens your mind to things you may not have thought of, especially as they're often coming from different standpoints and career routes to you. It's a reverse learning which can allow you to constantly reflect and improve your own skill set. I mentor multiple people in any one year, as many as I can fit in around my other obligations, and I learn something from every single one. As a mentor, my job is to listen and to help them understand what they are essentially asking themselves, rather than to provide advice.

Travel

Travel opens your mind, changes your perspective, and broadens your horizons, literally as well as figuratively. I would advise anyone starting out in their career to take any opportunities for travel when they arise. Though not an option that is open to everyone, it is a great way to learn about yourself. There is something about the familiarity of our regular existence that limits our exploration and therefore our understanding of our capabilities.

The challenge is to be sufficiently removed, mentally if not physically, from the rhythms of our normal day-to-day existence and to push ourselves out of our comfort zone. The simple encountering of new cultures and people encourages the development of interpersonal skills, allows you to use skills you haven't yet recognised and reveals sides to your character that have been untested in the familiarity of home. I hadn't thought of myself as a powerful or particularly persistent communicator in my early career, but when travelling in Ecuador and presented with an angry bus driver who was tossing luggage left, right and centre, I was forced to find my voice, using my most basic Spanish, to appeal to him to put mine back, to avoid having my luggage dumped by the side of the road at a stop far from my planned destination. Likewise, I didn't think I was the most creative of people when it came to drama, and I didn't get any big parts in the school plays. However, my ability to deliver an award-winning mime was the only thing that convinced a bus driver to stop his bus full of chickens as we rode down a steep mountain pass in Indonesia, saving my pride when I suddenly experienced a severe bout of nausea and needed to get off. I am sure you can appreciate my relief on that one!

Trivial as these examples are, they demonstrate how we can overlook capabilities when viewing them through the lens of our immediate environments. Change your scenery, challenge yourself, step out of the day to day, and you might just uncover more about yourself.

Commit to making time to reflect

Perhaps the least obvious of my recommendations for improving your self-awareness is to get into the habit of practising. Whether this is freeing up time in your agenda to simply reflect, or looking out the window in order to daydream a little, it's important to find the time. This is something I now do regularly: my Friday afternoons have been blocked out for many years now with a 'blue sky thinking' commitment. I take time to reflect on the week and think about what worked, what didn't, what I could have done better and what priorities are now forming. I get rid of the things that I won't work on any more and make space for those that have bubbled up during the week and which are now going to take priority.

The point of having a regular date with yourself like this is to stop thinking about all of the stuff which easily fills our days and which stops us looking out to the future. It's an opportunity to consider the less predictable and the more unknown and check in with the person we have been that week. It's by taking time to do this exercise that you take control of the things that shape where you spend your time. It can be a great way to shape your goals or your priorities, and the more you do it, the easier it is to tune into what you think matters. As you check in with how you actually feel, it becomes easier to know when you are pushing against your own values. Doing it once a year is a start, whether through New Year's resolutions or the annual performance review. Hopefully your commitment to reflection will last longer than a New Year's resolution though! Those reflection habits that work are the ones that can be broken down into small steps, to become part of the rhythm of life, rather than a step change that is too hard to implement. Try to find a frequency that becomes a habit. Weekly look backs, like my Friday afternoons, maybe? Or you could try creating time to reflect after each meeting, if only fleetingly. Did you achieve what you needed? What could have been better? Reflection can soon become second nature, though it takes time to settle into a rhythm that works for you.

> **Reflection – Checking in**
> Looking back at the last month and your decisions around where to spend your time, was this consistent with what you value? Did you act in the way you wanted? Are there any patterns?

There are so many different ways for you to develop your self-awareness, there's no excuse not to try. Life deals us all a different hand of cards; looking at them, and understanding what you have or don't have, will prepare you for that game that lies ahead. But it doesn't end there. The art of self-awareness lies in accepting this is a continuous journey. Some skills can change, new ones will emerge, our desires change and, as life progresses, likely so will our goals. On the other hand, some things like our personalities or our drive will remain constant. Recognising this and choosing how to accept or change the various elements is what puts you in a powerful position to get the best out of yourself and to unleash your unique power. The more you practise this, the easier it will be, and the goal is to make it second nature. Once you know where you are and who you are, life events or big changes may force you to reevaluate, but if you have a grasp on the process and have made it second nature, you will adapt.

Step 3: Give shape to what you want to achieve

Most of the elements in the product map, the things that make up who we are, are inherited, and the challenge is to recognise, accept, interpret and leverage (or manage) them as we progress through our careers by developing our self-awareness. These are givens, call them attributes if you like, that we need to work with. These will change or evolve as your career continues. Each experience, learning or training you undertake will shape you. You are, essentially, eternally evolving. The piece that completes the jigsaw is the goals that you set for yourself, giving voice to what you want and aspire to do or be. This is a *choice*, not a given. Your passion and values can be enough to give you a sense of direction, one that defines what you see as important and hence where you gravitate to, but having an idea of what you want to accomplish, a picture in your mind, will give you the focus to take steps to follow through. Here is a fun way to uncover your desires or aspirations.

Visualise it

There is a lot to be said for creating an image of something to help you recognise and strive towards it. Daydreaming, though often dismissed as a non-valuable pastime, is actually a very useful, albeit abstract, way of understanding your ambitions, perhaps in a way you may not have thought about them before. I've used a technique similar to daydreaming in many team workshops, coaching sessions and even in a full amphitheatre at a career fair. It helps people define goals that they would *like* to have or put dimensions on goals that they already have within them. It can help you conjure up descriptions of the types of job you may like or, indeed, the type of culture you would enjoy working in. I continue to encourage people to build even the briefest of moments into their agendas every week to simply look out of the window and stare. Much like the aforementioned period of weekly reflection, the action of simply having a moment of thought to yourself – when you tune out the noise of day-to-day business – helps you to continually remind yourself of what's important and see things further out than the immediate activity that surrounds our daily lives.

Take a moment to do the following exercise. See if it evokes something different to the goals that you hold in your mind today, in particular with regard to your career.

EXERCISE – IDENTIFYING BIG PICTURE GOALS

Close your eyes and imagine a moment some years into the future. You are a successful individual, content in what you do, and you have balance and pleasure in your life. You're surrounded by the people and the things that make you happy, and you have a sense of fulfilment. On this particular evening, in your mind, you've been invited to an awards ceremony. Picture yourself attending this ceremony. You have been invited along with your nearest and dearest to pick up an award. You see yourself getting ready for this award, surrounding by all the trappings of a flourishing career. You have indeed been extremely successful. You head off to the awards ceremony in a car which was sent to your house to pick you up; such is the status you have achieved in your particular environment. You spend the evening surrounded by people that you respect and like to be around and whom you look up to. They are all there to share in this moment. As you receive the award, you give a short speech thanking key people for helping you on this journey. You talk about the challenges you overcame to accomplish such an achievement. It makes you feel very proud. You thoroughly enjoyed the evening and return home to your family. A couple of days later, you share in the celebration around the table over a meal together. As you recount the story to people close to you, you have a real sense of pride. You recall not only that evening but the process that got you to that point. Enjoy the moment; revel in how it feels. You really have done exceedingly well. It's everything you thought about doing but didn't dare imagine was possible.

Close your eyes and feel it for a few minutes longer before reading on.

Capture how you feel and dwell on that moment. What do you see? Who are you grateful to and for what? Be sure to build this picture out and capture it. Are you smiling?

While reading this, have you been able to conjure up that scenario in your mind? To derive from that picture a goal or ambition, if you are unsure of your direction, ask yourself the following three questions:

- What was the award for?
- What were the things you were most proud of?
- Who were you surrounded by on the two evenings?

Note what the answers are and if this points you to a goal. If so, try and describe what that goal is, remembering to include by when will it be complete.

This simple exercise works for framing what you would like success to be in your career too, in the event that you are struggling to define that through logical thought processes. Setting yourself goals once you have an ideal in mind, though not strictly self-awareness, is key to understanding how you may seek to change or indeed leverage all the elements of your product map. (If this tool worked for you, there are additional exercises at the end of the book which cover values and team environments.)

Holding on to what you decide is important, what you set for yourself as goals, in a world of change and adversaries, is challenging. Having taken the time to reflect on who you are in more detail, you will have a stronger idea of where your individual powers lie and whether you are heading in a direction that works for you. You might, as was the case for me, be only slightly aware, missing key pieces of information, and needing a rethink on direction. Remember that you will change as an individual and reflection is ongoing. What is important is that you are now starting to become aware and you are equipped to handle it: you know who you are. Holding on to or being 'who you are' is the next challenge.

2

Be Yourself – Mirror Two

B EING YOURSELF means living according to your values as you pursue your goals in life. Simple if you know what they are, surely? So why do so few people do it? Let's look closer.

Like many parents, I took great joy in story time with my two children, especially when they were young. One day, I was reading them the classic fairy tale of Snow White; we were at the part of the story which describes how the Evil Queen gazes into the magic mirror each day, asking it who is the fairest in the land, and receiving the reassurance that, of course, she was! Until one day... 'Oh Queen, Snow White is the fairest in the land!' Ouch, what a slap in the face. These few simple words send the Evil Queen into meltdown. However, it's my eldest son's reaction which stays with me. He asked me to wait and turn back a page, looking very carefully at the two illustrations of the Queen gazing into the mirror before and after the answer changed. I wasn't sure what he was looking for until he said to me: 'But Mummy, nothing's changed! She still looks the same!' He made an excellent point that, to this day, I still find poignant – nothing about the Queen's appearance *had* changed. The only thing that was different was that she was told that, in comparison to someone else, she wasn't good enough; she was somehow less.

Do not absorb everything

Now, of course, this isn't the perfect example. Siding even momentarily with the villain of the story. I'd say that *Snow White* has a few different 'morals' that it promotes – some of which are still propagated today, and some of which may not be lessons we want to keep – but there's something in it, nonetheless. Just like the Evil Queen, we don't like being told we are not good enough, smart enough or strong enough, and comparing ourselves to others is a quick way to ruin our day. However, it takes a lot of self-belief and self-control to be able to turn off other people's opinions or stop looking at and comparing yourself to the people near you.

This is where the second mirror comes in. You are the only person in your reflection, and you can take control of what you want to see. Light bounces off a mirror's surface, changed by the angle you choose to look at it, and neither it nor your eyes absorb everything. A mirror, and how you use it, is *selective*. In other words, it is not enough for us to know what we're good at, what we value, what we are aiming for and what we love; we also need to be able to hold on to these things while reflecting away negativity, falseness or the confidence-eroding stuff that seeks to challenge it.

So, how does this work, having just been extolling the virtues of listening to feedback? This is still true – it will do you no good at all to close your eyes and ears and refuse to take anything in. However, it is important to be selective about how you use what you hear. It's about self-belief and how we build it, how we defend or utilise it, and how we maintain it while working with and among other people. At the end of the day, a career is, for most of us, going to involve working with people, through people and for people. As crucial as feedback is, the art of self-belief is knowing when to hold on to something despite others' opinions, with all the stubbornness of a piece of chewing gum stuck to your shoe. It's about knowing who to listen to and ignoring the trolls and the critics. It is about letting go of the ideas, and even sometimes the people, who seek to burden rather than encourage you.

Imagine where we would be today if everyone's belief in themselves sunk simply because people said they were no good? Apparently, Walt Disney was criticised early in his career by his editor at the *Kansas City Star* for, 'Lacking imagination and having no good ideas'.[3] Albert Einstein, according to some biographers, didn't speak until he was four or read until the age of seven, both slower than average, but he went on to change the world.[4] And then there are the famous artists who seldom achieve great success until after they die. There's Vincent van Gogh who, rumour would have us believe, sold one painting while alive, and that was, by all accounts, to his brother.[5] Had Van Gogh listened to the silent dismissal of his talent that an absence of sales conveys, the world would have been denied one of the best artists of all time. The skill in utilising feedback *effectively*, or choosing to acknowledge it but not action it verbatim, is a fine art.

Being yourself takes practice, but it's worth it

Possessing a great understanding of yourself, hard as that is, will not benefit you or the world unless you are able to *be* yourself too. It takes effort, at least initially, to just be yourself because, surprisingly, it's not second nature. We have learned so many ways to do what society expects of us or what others expect, and we are constantly exposed to marketing messages telling us what we should be, or do, or wear, or playing on our insecurities to get us to buy things. As humans, being part of a group or having a certain identity feels safe, so depending on how much you 'hide' or cover up your true self, it may take practice to stand apart and do your own thing because it can feel like a risk.

But that's the beauty of it; with the self-awareness you have learnt to build, you can actively *choose* when to stand out and when to blend in or go with the flow. This is far more valuable than allowing your subconscious to dictate how you behave without you knowing about it. The value goes beyond your own gain too.

Bringing diverse perspectives

Knowing and being yourself helps diversity to flourish. If you aren't able to understand and be your true self, and you try instead to be what you think people want, then you will not let your unique perspective come through. Your teams or company will miss out on the element of diversity that you bring – what a loss!

We know that the power of diversity is not realised by simply getting balanced representations of people around a table; this is essential, but it's not enough. We only realise the benefits of a diverse group when we ensure that diverse contributions can be made. We have to make sure that diverse people are not just *there*, but that they are actively included and able to make their contributions. And there are different kinds of diversity too; it's not just about race and gender (although these are, of course, very important). Diversity covers a whole range of things. There's inherent diversity, which means the characteristics and context we are born with, like nationality, sexual orientation, race and age. Then we have acquired diversity; these might include views that are shaped by our experiences, countries we have lived in, companies, life events, religion and so on. Finally, we have *cognitive diversity*, which essentially means the schools of thought we have grown through, the academic institutions we have been influenced by and the ways in which we think (problem-solving styles, creativity styles, logic and lateral thinking). All of these unique facets of you can add to a team's diversity and you will all be stronger as a result, so use it!

In 2011, I headed up the acquisition of the company Kamis, a Polish company. As the new CEO, I was the only person from the acquiring company to sit on the board, and I hadn't set foot in Poland before taking the role. As I adapted to the new language and culture, and as I sought to integrate the company into the US-owned acquirer, I had a choice: I could fit in, observe and adopt how things were already done, or I could look, listen and then decide how to use the differences that I brought with me to shape a forward path.

On the surface, as a board, we looked very similar: a pretty even gender split and all of us were white. Our physical diversity was not of great note. However, I had grown up in completely different companies and I was shaped by different experiences, and so too were each of my valued board members. Although it was hard – even hostile – in the short term, the fact that I looked at things differently and brought challenges to the table was eventually seen as bold and creative. Being myself – with tact but without compromise – gave me some staunch supporters and, I dare say, some enemies too, round the board table. On the other side, the local knowledge, extraordinary work ethic, tenacity and resourcefulness that came from my board counterparts were definite assets, and I would have been short-sighted to ignore them in favour of my way of doing things. In maintaining our diversity and combining our differences, we gave the company the best of both worlds and created an environment that worked for everyone.

Thankfully, we are at a moment where there is increasingly more momentum towards building an equitable society, realising the value of diversity and cultivating inclusive environments. This should help people to feel comfortable being themselves. There has never been a better moment to drop what is not working for you and shine as you are.

The path of least resistance

Being yourself can also be a boost to your personal productivity. Let me give you an example. When I was having my first child, I was a managing director, working in a pattern dictated by my not-so-distant single life, recent marriage, social priorities and my career ambition. I did wonder how I would be able to fit in the job, as I knew it, alongside a child. Yet, ironically, having children was the biggest productivity gain I have had in my career to date. I didn't have time to be anyone else but myself, nor to worry what people thought too much! Suddenly my priorities were clearer, and I didn't waste time on some of the more trivial decision-making. I didn't fret when I turned up with milk on my shoulder. I had a moment to recast my expectations with the team to allow the adjustment in my behaviour and pattern to become the norm for me. Essentially, I stopped trying so hard.

Make it more than just good intentions

Being yourself takes self-control. The recent focus on wellness and work-life integration forces many people to evaluate where they spend their time. Many younger people, in my teams of recent years, tell me how much they care about having a different balance to their life, and that they don't want to be 'confined' by their job. It is therefore surprising, or perhaps disappointing, to see how many of them can sometimes be hooked to the desk late into the evening, working weekend hours, which haven't been expressly required of them.

I was no stranger to working late, or sometimes doing work on the weekend, until I realised how out of sync with my values it was. In the early years of my career, when technology was such that your desk computer remained at work and you left the office for the evening or the weekend, it was easier to not take work with you. I occasionally had to go to work on a Sunday for a specific task, but these times were few and far between.

With the advances in technology today, fuelled by the possibilities of remote working that the COVID-19 pandemic of 2020-2021 highlighted, it's going to require discipline to stick to those same principles. The point here is that it's not about your personal time management, or work-life partitioning, it's a question as to whether you are behaving in ways that match up with what you say is important to you. If not, is that because you don't feel you can or because you just haven't thought about it in practice?

> **Reflection – Is your work aligned with your values?**
> Does your pattern of work reflect what you believe is important? Are you aware of how you prioritise where you spend time? Could you make any easy changes to align these more?

We all evolve along our career journeys, and so you should expect things about you to change. As you succeed in being yourself, you will adapt, you will be happier, you will attract the right people and, importantly, you'll deepen your self-belief and self-control, both of which will take you towards fulfilling your goals.

Failure is our friend

Truly being yourself not only means deflecting away negative influences; it also means dropping conditioned beliefs and fear-based thinking by respecting and accepting yourself. This is critical for self-esteem and should feel empowering. What often stands in the way is the fear of failure and the idea that perfection is the goal.

What do large tech companies, successful entrepreneurs and scientists have in common? They all embrace and learn from failure; some actively invite it. We are so used to seeing the successes in life that we seldom appreciate the failures that precede them. For every consumer product launched, roughly one in 10 will be successful. Similarly, many inventions only come about as the result of an insight from the failure of another product or service that would otherwise have gone undiscovered. Why then do we not embrace that same acceptance and curiosity when it comes to our own lives and, indeed, our careers?

When I studied engineering, one module required us to build model bridges complete with concrete and reinforced steel structures. In order to learn about the capability of the bridge, we tested it until it 'failed', then analysed the way it had collapsed. The learning wasn't apparent until the failure happened. Failure is a powerful source of learning, yet we seem reluctant to embrace it proactively in our careers and personal lives. I learnt about the types of company, job content and even management styles that work for me by feeling the pain of the ones that didn't.

Imagine if the effort we put into recovering from failure was far less than the effort it takes to try and avoid failure, and it also taught us something in the process? But that is often the case. Here's a real example to illustrate. As I began to work with automation, there were many new programme launches, some with a large impact on how we would work. As a general manager with a business to run, I found myself putting a great deal of effort into pushing back when technical features didn't quite fit my business area and might impact the customer experience. That was until I understood the lesson of efficiency. For the software engineers, the aim was to break the system as fast as possible and to then understand what exceptions needed fixing before scaling. No rollout was ever perfect, but the team were laser focused on looking for where and how it failed and then modifying. This way, they could scale far faster. Had they waited for a perfect solution to be ready first, they would never have begun and it would have been worse for customers long-term. Now take that lesson into your career. Rather than avoid going for a new job or embarking on a dream career because there may be bumps along the road, try and accept these bumps and tackle them, one at a time, to create the potential to move forward.

Equally, in each job, don't play it too safe and avoid risks. Instead, take the risks and have a plan B to get back on track. I have created strategies for many business units and have had to go back to the drawing board on a number of occasions when things just didn't work out. I've missed sales targets, lost customers and mismanaged expectations, but without exception I have learned as a consequence and the world didn't end! What hurts your pride at the time makes you stronger in the long run.

So, as you look at yourself, try and see the value in failure rather than seeing it as a shortcoming to be avoided at all costs. That way, you let go of the fear. Once you can view failure as a valid option, there is no room for the pursuit of perfection.

Your definition of success is what matters

If you are measuring yourself against someone else's definition of success, you will never be satisfied. You can decide for yourself what success in your career, or indeed your life, looks like, remembering that this too can change over time.

In my previous example of early motherhood, I, like most new mothers, was handling the biggest challenge life had thrown at me; keeping a new little life safe without an instruction manual, when a self-assembly chest complete with manual still defeats many avid DIYers! I was adjusting in my job and juggling the new world of competitive childcare as both my husband and I worked at that point, all while keeping my sanity. For me, that was succeeding!

On my first business trip away, I was reading a newspaper article which talked about how women couldn't have it all. In particular, it assured me that we women couldn't be doing a day job while fulfilling the mother or carer role at home without making major compromises and failing at both. This was my modern-day, fairy-tale mirror, telling me I was no good, and not even offering a comparison I was failing to measure up to.

When I started out in my career, and looked up the ranks to see what success 'looked like', what I saw were predominantly male individuals at the top of companies. They were seldom under 50, many had lost their hair, their fitness or figures, and no small number had lost their spouses, families and health. I don't consider that to be an attractive example of success at all! Now, although I am the 'wrong' side of 50, I value my health, my family, my sanity and my fitness. I eat healthily, feel good about the way my body works and looks, and I try to sleep well. Yes, I may dither about some trivial things like what shoes to wear in the morning, but I'm OK with that. What I'm not doing is adhering to any stereotypical image of a leader, nor leading a company by behaving in the same way that I thought I needed to in my early career – so does that make me unsuccessful? Of course not.

My definition of success is what matters to me, and your definition of success is what should matter to you. Don't start with other people's ideas as limits around which you must carve your ambitions. Despite all the op-eds about how women 'can't have it all', I am a mum, a wife, a friend and also a successful businesswoman and social tennis doubles partner. This, for me, is the epitome of what success means. To live and maintain it, I have found a way of managing the balance that works. You can do this too, to achieve whatever your own picture of success is; don't listen to the naysayers, but believe in your own priorities. Whether it is simply wanting to make sure you can surf every Tuesday at 4pm, or going skateboarding with a pet Komodo dragon on a Saturday at 2am, go for it! Who is anyone to tell you that's not what success looks like? It's about achieving the things that *you* would like to do and ensuring the priorities you have in life are not undone by others' perception of success.

> **Reflection – Perceptions of success**
> Can you think of what success looks like for you? Are you able to work towards it? If anything is stopping you, can you think how you could change it?

Share your story to encourage others

Generic or stereotypical feedback and opinions are all around you, and they are seldom helpful. In my work driving diversity, as a working parent and a woman in STEM (science, technology, engineering and maths), I have been increasingly vocal in recent years, and where possible, I have used my role and its visibility to share that message with women or other individuals who have similar challenges. I encourage everyone to share their story so that the world of work has a variety of role models for everyone. This 'ask' goes beyond women to everyone in positions of responsibility, from underrepresented groups to anyone succeeding despite the adversity they face. It won't always be easy. I have written articles in the mainstream press, and it still surprises me that it is often the readers that you are trying to help who don't believe your version of success can be possible; those who have listened to the naysayers for too long and who try to bring you down with their negative comments. Habits take a long time to change, so all efforts to do this help!

Own even your smallest of choices

When you get into the details, it's surprising how many elements of our lives are defined or shaped by the desire to please others, or just to fit in. This is apparent in the subconscious things we do and the habits we have, perhaps even more so than in the conscious choices we make. As you take control of what you want to do with your life and your career, it's good to reflect on where you might have choices that perhaps don't seem like choices; the habits, rituals and values that you have so far taken for granted. Often, we cause many of the stresses in our own lives by trying to keep up with our own perception of what 'good' looks like, and we don't always question why or how we came to hold some of those perceptions.

Let me give you a simple example around keeping house. My husband works from home, which gives us a great deal of flexibility for which I am very grateful. We don't have a nanny, and we share the housework and childcare responsibilities, the administration and the repairs. It is our own set of choices. We have chosen to ask for help from each other. Having relocated between countries four times since having kids, my husband and I don't have the luxury of a close family and support network around us, but we have learned, very explicitly, where we can rely on each other.

Where I save time now is on the small things which habit would have me overlook. I don't iron any of my children's clothes, as they don't actually need it – they'll be rumpled within minutes of wearing them anyway. I no longer iron sheets or towels, although I grew up believing this was a necessary chore. Of course, this is made easy for me because I don't mind what people think of my children's clothes and can live with a slightly crumpled sheet! These are seemingly trivial choices, but the point is that I had to question them or I would have carried on doing things the way I had while growing up. Every day I wake up and make a conscious choice about what I'm going to care about and what I'm going to do. This is not always going to be what other people expect, and that is OK.

Take a moment to question the things in your routine and whether or not they add value to your life. Ask whether or not you would notice if you stop doing them and also whether you do them because of what other people may think of you. Then we can translate this idea into work.

The first time I accepted not being able to read every single email, it was hugely uncomfortable. I worried people would think my attention was slipping. I cut back, and instead of doing everything, I let some things go. Nobody noticed. All that worry I'd had about this reflecting badly on my performance was in my head. I had a perception that was not aligned with reality. Interestingly, that trial gave me freedom to test things out and to understand where I was doing things because they *were* necessary, rather than doing them because I *believed* they were needed.

What are the small choices you can make that may free up some time and energy? For example – do you really need to read and respond to *every* email you get? Even the automated ones, the newsletters and the closing-the-loop thank yous? Today, I try not to be a hostage to my email and accept I will not get everything in my inbox done, so I focus on trying to recognise the important stuff rather than trying to process everything. Nowadays, my 'out of office' tells people their email will be deleted, and if important or urgent, how they can get assistance. It is amazing how effective that one small change can be! Have a look at what you could do differently. It takes courage to challenge habits, but there's no reason not to try.

Reflection – Questioning habits
Can you think of a few things that you do, habits you have adopted, without questioning why? Are they really

helpful to you? Could you drop or reduce these without anyone noticing?

Let's talk about confidence

It always strikes me as astounding how many very capable people describe themselves as not confident. Research shows 79% of women and 62% of men have a challenge with their confidence in the workplace.[6] It takes confidence to be yourself, and the lack of it can be a significant stumbling block for people. If self-belief is *trusting* that you have the capabilities to achieve your dreams or goals – as identified with the exercises on self-awareness – then self-confidence is bringing that belief through in your *actions*. There are varying schools of thought on strict definitions of what confidence is and how to get it, but my point of view is this: that confidence is not just a characteristic you have. It is the product of a skill you can learn *and* the environment or situation you're in. By seeing confidence with a situational lens, as opposed to seeing it as a fixed characteristic, you give yourself a stronger chance of improving it and changing your perception of yourself for the better – boosting your self-esteem in the process.

Let me give you an example. Now, I consider myself to be a reasonably confident individual at work. However, there are situations where that isn't the case. When I had my first child, I was definitely not what I would describe as a confident new mum! However, did I learn to grow in confidence as I adapted to my new reality? Absolutely. Similarly, when I moved to Poland, I didn't speak the language or know the culture and, since being a female CEO was not that common, I felt like I was a curiosity. I was not confident when I started this challenge. However, again, I grew quickly and adapted to my new situation with help and support.

Wherever your comfort zone is in terms of confidence, let me challenge you to look at it not as something you categorically have or don't have, but as something which you can achieve and work at to improve – especially with a good support network around you.

In order to get more comfortable and gain confidence, it helps to recognise the moments when you feel you lack confidence and identify the fears that sit behind it. Maybe it is driven by situations or even by certain individuals? It is a personal thing, so you need to be honest with yourself. It may also require you to identify past conditioning and seek proof to dispel the negative perception you may be carrying and reinforce the positive ones you have. You may even find it worthwhile talking to someone to help you tease out the patterns of what makes you feel confident or not. Coaches and counsellors are trained to help people reflect on this kind of question.

Challenge your own perspective

As I was practising some public speaking at school, I was given a helpful tip from my dad who was an English drama teacher. He told me that even the best actors get nervous or anxious waiting in the wings, and it is this anxiety that makes them perform better. I speak regularly today and, indeed, I still get that wave of nervousness. But, instead of recognising it as fear and lack of confidence – as I know many people do when it comes to public speaking – I see it as the boost I need to do my best. Perhaps you can rethink the things that you associate with lack of confidence and see if this shift in mindset could help?

Should you 'fake it until you make it', as the saying goes? This is the age-old idea that you can succeed by pretending to have confidence and, in doing so, find it. It's a piece of advice that I think should have a caveat. On the positive side, if this is what it takes to get over the initial anxiety holding you back, then great. The downside is that this is focused on displaying confidence to others and thus prioritising what they think. If it is indeed fake, then by definition, it means being someone you are not. Only if you convert this to actual confidence, that *you* have in *yourself* over time, is this really a win. The risk is that, if you continue to behave in a way that is not *you*, and that becomes how you make progress, then it will be more difficult to drop this 'act' later on, as you will have come to rely on it. Perhaps find a way to extend your confidence by seeing this same idea as stepping outside of your comfort zone, trying something new and being in control of those actions. In that way, they are never 'fake'.

There is indeed merit in the idea that you can get or build what you want by believing it first, summed up nicely in this quote on self-belief often attributed to Henry Ford: 'Whether you think you can or you think you can't, you are right.'[7] So, try to flip the 'faking it' from a negative to a positive. How about, 'Believe it to achieve it!'

Don't beat yourself up about lack of confidence either. Almost everyone will struggle to feel confident during at least one point in their life. You're not alone.

Careful not to overcompensate for insecurities

Many people are highly confident in some areas, which compensates for lacking confidence or being insecure in others, and understanding both is key. Examining the past and accepting where you are at is so fundamental to moving forward and unshackling yourself from self-limiting thoughts. As a young girl at school, I gained my confidence in my abilities because I could see the results of my exams in black and white. Exam results gave me hard evidence that I should be confident in my abilities. I didn't derive the same confidence when it came to interactions involving people's perceptions. I took what evidence I found and shaped my thoughts – not always positively.

I can still remember how it felt being sent to the school nurse on a weekly basis to take part in a dieting programme at age 13 – hard evidence of a 'failing'. It's understandable, then, that I developed image problems. Then, in a year out before university, I worked on tunnel engineering projects underground in dark and poor lighting. After three months, the lead tunneller, an Irishman, exclaimed one day as I set my laser target up in the tunnelling shield, 'By Jeez, it's a girl!' If I wasn't even recognisable as a woman, on top of the earlier weight problem, no wonder my self-esteem took a monumental hit. With those two negative experiences, it is hardly surprising that I focused on the things that I was confident in but too much so! This is not the right counter move. Trying to balance out areas of low confidence by investing all your efforts into areas of higher confidence brings its own set of challenges. Only in recent years did I focus on disproving the 'hard evidence' gathered in my formative years and work on the healthier goal of not leaving my self-esteem in the hands of others.

On the other end of the scale, overconfidence is something to be wary of, as it too can be a limitation. The trick is to recognise your feelings, which brings us back to the art of self-awareness again. Remember, everyone has this challenge to some extent, just related to different things. With practice, you can be in control of your confidence levels and adapt to each new situation successfully.

> **Reflection – Barriers to confidence**
> Can you think of situations where you are very confident and then some where you are not? What is the big difference between the two? Is there an actual hurdle to remove or just one that you perceive? How can you change this? What small steps can you take?

Your personal 'volume' switch

Like confidence, there is a balance to strike in using all your capabilities and characteristics to become more 'you'. The overuse of a strength becomes a weakness; recognising but not living according to your values may actually reduce your self-esteem; and actions that compensate for insecurities, rather than dispelling the negative beliefs, can leave you vulnerable to new limiting behaviours. Finding the right amount of 'flex' requires practice and patience. This is something I struggled with and, in most cases, the compensating action was driven from a place of insecurity and a desire to please and be 'perfect'. The messages I received of how I was perceived by different stakeholders (and from probably hundreds of hints from my mum and dad many years earlier, all of which I ignored), was not always how I saw myself, and it required some adjustment.

There are parts of myself – particularly my confidence and unwillingness to fade into the background – that can come off as aggressive or intimidating if I let them play out unchecked and at full volume in all circumstances. Likewise, there will be aspects of your personality that are more helpful and appropriate in some circumstances and less so in others.

This is a lesson I had to learn and a skill I had to develop. I now look at my ability to adapt my behaviour for different audiences as 'turning the volume switch up or down' on my personality. It helps to instil this concept as a mental picture. This concept can be applied to any skills and elements on your product map where there is a tendency for you to overcompensate or where more nuance in different situations would be helpful. For example, a tendency towards leadership which is overused could be bossiness; a helper tendency could lead to burnout; and confidence in public speaking, wrongly applied, could lead to drowning out diverse voices.

If understanding your 'product' is one level of self-awareness, controlling how you use elements within it, to adapt to situations and different people, is a whole new and advanced level. It is your self-belief and self-control working in harmony, and it's an invaluable skill.

Succeeding at being yourself means being aware of, and in control of, the 'volume switch' for your many dimensions. Giving thought to how you want to go about being yourself and swapping out the mask for a finely tuned dial is your challenge.

Figure 2.1 below provides a few simple prompts to help you note your current status and challenge yourself to be more 'you', where necessary. If you answer 'yes' to any of these, well done for being brave and honest. To move forward, assign yourself one simple step you will take to improve the status quo. Often, the process of articulating with honesty what is holding us back can be the most powerful enabler.

From ignoring the trolls, to accepting yourself, acknowledging your past and being open to constructive feedback, it all takes time. Being honest with what is important to you and ensuring that this is not forgotten among the many trade-offs you make will give you a guiding star. This will help you be who you are and allow you to shine as yourself. Once you are in control of that, you are well placed to take on the many challenges that life throws at you while you continue to be yourself.

FIGURE 2.1: QUESTION LIST: ARE YOU BEING YOURSELF?

Understand	Yes/No	Action
Do you know what success looks like for you in your career and life?		
Do you 'wear a mask' to work or do you show your whole self?		
If you do 'wear a mask', can you express what is stopping you from being 'you' and what would have to change?		
Do you have habits that no longer support your values?		
Can you express what fears may be harming your confidence?		
Can you recognise when you overcompensate for lack of confidence and what you do in practice?		

3

Context – The Cheetah

UNPACKING AND owning all that is your 'self' is a necessary step. However, on its own it is still incomplete knowledge and insufficient to help you navigate your career. You will move through many situations in your career where the context differs, and this can be tough to read and incorporate effectively.

Let's meet the cheetah. What I particularly like about this svelte, feline animal, prowling around on a dry plain in sub-Saharan Africa, eyeing up its large prey, is its size versus the size and sheer number of wildebeest. On the face of it, success for the cheetah looks unlikely. The cheetah is, however, acutely aware of her strengths and her weaknesses, and she uses these to gauge the situation strategically. Should the cheetah get the *context* of the situation wrong, it is genuinely a matter of life and death. In hunting for food for her young offspring, the cheetah must also put herself in danger, so it's very important that she understands the situation and plays it to her advantage.

The cheetah is the fastest land animal, capable of going from 0 to 60mph (97 km/h), in under three seconds. She can reach speeds of 75mph (121km/h). However, she can only keep this up for about 20 seconds, beyond which she will simply burn out. So, being aware of this capability, and its fundamental limitation, is critical. The cheetah relies on her ability to carefully analyse each situation before making any moves, ensuring she has time and distance to launch her attack. Importantly, when the cheetah feels that she may not have everything she needs for a successful hunt, and that the danger to her may be too high, she accepts this and moves on to a different environment in search of alternative lunch arrangements.

There's a lesson to be learnt in this image, I think, about how important the impact of *different environments and conditions* can be on our ability to leverage our strengths and weaknesses. Particularly about what can happen when conditions don't support us.

If it was only about the strengths and weaknesses of the cheetah, she would simply lie down and have a rest after putting on an impressive burst of speed for 20 seconds, and not have to worry about being eaten herself. However, the hunting ground doesn't work like that and, in reality, there is a calculation or a trade-off needed in each moment. In the animal kingdom, that skill is obviously second nature, but for us humans, who are not used to it, particularly when it comes to our careers, it takes a lot of practice and understanding to read the environment.

It requires patience to see the conditions and changes and to know if, how and when to adapt to them. Above all, I think it takes bravery to know when to walk away from something rather than to continue.

Context affects everything

The metaphor of the cheetah is about understanding that your environment, and everything in it, impacts you. Placing yourself in an environment that plays to your strengths and meets your needs will ultimately be more rewarding. It is about learning how to recognise what conditions you need for success, then recognising when things change and how that affects those conditions. Both are needed to be able to respond to change effectively. This means being adaptable as well, something which we will explore in detail in the next chapter. Let me give you an example of when I felt the power of context.

When I returned from my second maternity leave, I accepted a new role which was similar in size to the one I had prior to my leave but back in my home country and based in HQ. The reality of returning to the head office environment, in a familiar country, meant that I missed some of the challenge and the change I had thrived on out in the markets. In the new role, some of my skills were also not as necessary and I could feel that something was missing. In accepting this position, I let go of a job where I was alive; one that was complicated, risky, relentless and full of so many different people and stakeholders. It was strangely both energising and exhausting in one. In the move, I had traded the pace and excitement of a developing capital city for a comparatively sleepy, country village. It was a stark contrast.

Now, I hadn't changed, but so much of my work context had, and I didn't factor this into my decision making when taking the role. I had failed, up to that point, to really appreciate the role of *context* in my fulfilment.

Things do change, so recognising what you need and adapting keeps you powerful. It was a tough lesson for me but one that I valued extremely highly.

Why does context matter?

Context matters because it shapes the conditions for success. Each of us operates differently, and we respond to different combinations of external factors in different ways. Context can affect the way in which we use our skills and indeed their impact. Imagine someone who is brilliant when working under an autonomous manager, or even no manager at all, who then has to work for a very controlling, hands-on micromanager; or someone who needs the energy of a team and falters working in isolation; or someone who has worked in an individual office suddenly presented with an open plan environment. In these situations, nothing changes in their product map, their confidence or their resolve to be themselves. Rather, the context doesn't support it – in this case, the potential elements of *work style.* The resulting impact on fulfilment and happiness can be such that individuals may not want to continue in that job, and things quickly head downhill.

The context of our careers is not something we give as much thought to as we might do for our skills or ambitions, but the cost of not giving it consideration can be high.

> **Reflection – Changes in context**
> Have you experienced a situation where all was fine at work and you were feeling fulfilled and then suddenly you weren't? What did you notice that was different? Can you link this to a change in your context?

So, just what *are* the elements that make up the context of your work world? What does change look like, and can you detect it as it happens or even before it happens?

Choose contexts to meet needs

Your *context* is defined as the conditions that make up your work situation; the things that influence you day to day. It is made up of many layers. It goes beyond the physical environment and the pay cheque. These are some of the common components to consider:

- Location – geography
- Location – commute
- Physical environment
- Company culture
- Organisational structure
- Manager
- Team composition
- Communication framework
- Benefits and flexibility
- Unwritten 'rules'
- Job scope
- Reward structure
- Development and new opportunities
- Inclusivity and feeling of belonging

All these elements of context can vary from job to job and even over time in the same job. As individuals, we have expectations from employment relating to the *job*, the *manager* and the *company*, yet, often, the focus is on securing the more tangible elements of physical environment and compensation. Your success or failure, or indeed your satisfaction, however, can often lie more within the other elements noted in the list. Taking ownership of your career means deciding which elements are important to you and also what combination or balance of these elements you need in order to grow and have a successful and fulfilling experience.

And this is all while recognising that many of these elements are not expressly agreed in contracts.

If you are early on in your career and you don't yet have a great deal of experience in multiple environments, it's good to think about which elements might affect your contentment and which of these can change, some of which you may not yet have thought of. You can begin to imagine your ideal scenario and the context you would like to have. However, if you've had a number of different roles, you may already be able to see which elements made a real difference to you. You begin to see which things you *need*.

Everyone will have their own non-negotiable elements from the previous list, usually in terms of the contractual bits, but the elements of context that ensure you are feeling valued, challenged or just fulfilled do not always get the same logical consideration. On the face of it, the preceding list might look complicated, but you'll notice how you can quite easily identify where you may have firm requirements on the more tangible elements like benefits, remuneration or flexible working, and perhaps the practicalities of travelling or maximum commuting time, but less so on the rest.

The more experience you get, the more you will understand the impact and importance for you of these less obvious elements, like different styles of management, different working cultures or even different teams.

Start by noting down which factors are of importance to you, perhaps differentiating between the 'nice to haves' and the 'must haves'. Figure 3.1 gives an example of needs connected to job, manager and company. As you fill this out, ask yourself what your ideal job would have to contain for you to be fulfilled. Note these in the 'ideal' column. Try referring to your product map and ensure your needs incorporate and align with your values and working style etc. Then add the needs which are met for you today, in your current context. As you compare the needs you have in an ideal context with what you have today, you create an idea of how fulfilled you are in your current role.

FIGURE 3.1 NEEDS LIST – EXAMPLES

NEEDS	TODAY	IDEAL	MUST HAVE	NICE TO HAVE
	List	List	Y/N	Y/N
JOB	Challenge			
	People leadership			
	Change			
	Problem solving			
	External relationships			
	European remit			
	Salary level			
	Holidays			
MANAGER	Autonomy			
	Recognition			
	Experience to learn from Respect			
COMPANY	Vision I believe in			
	Brand or products I like			
	Location			
	Commute			
	Culture			
	Flexible working			
	Opportunities to grow			

In combination, all of these components are what you need to thrive. You can and should feel that these are choices you can make and seek to influence, just as compensation is. Whichever way you build the picture of what is right for you, it's sad but true that some of these elements may only become obvious as a 'need' when that need is not being met. This is one of the reasons I frequently advise people to move jobs early in their careers and try things out. You don't necessarily know, at the start of your career, what you may or may not like, but you can learn.

When the things you are passionate about also align with what you are good at, then you are more likely to perform well. So, if you are in pursuit of a more fulfilling career, there is merit in aligning your context and *needs* with your toolkit and your motivators. Having all your needs met makes you more contented. The opposite is also often true: when your needs are not met, it can lead to frustration. The key to maintaining balance is seeing any changes coming and adapting.

Spotting when things are not right

When your context is not right, you are not set up for success. As well as the increased likelihood of you delivering less than your best, or missing rewarding work projects, having a mismatched context can be a disappointment, a hang up and sometimes a real source of stress, if left unchecked.

Understanding the contexts in which you work best, and what your full needs are, is also tied to self-awareness. Being able to recognise when conditions are changing, and importantly, when you yourself are changing as a result of that, is essential if you are to keep your perspective and maintain healthy working habits. Most of us can recognise when we have had a bad day or a good day, but are you able to describe how work makes you feel or notice it on a daily basis?

Work environments can give you a boost or they can disappoint or burden you, and in the extreme, when they are far from what works for you, be that the tangible conditions like remuneration or the invisible tensions of a poor manager relationship, they can become a real problem. Sometimes, noticing that something is badly amiss happens only when it is entirely broken, and at other times it is a gradual loss of engagement or enthusiasm that creeps up on you.

In my early career, when I worked at Kraft Jacobs Suchard, I had all the variety a new graduate needed to explore what I liked. These experiences, exciting as they were for a newly-qualified engineer, helped me see that I was more excited by the commercial elements of the work. However, my attempt to move from the research and development (R&D) department into a commercial unit was initially met with resistance, the argument at the time being that I was 'an engineer and not a marketeer'.

I was not put off and continued to push, securing a mentor in the head of the R&D unit who, I am happy to say, eventually supported a move. Sadly, I was young and impatient, and when the agreement to transfer me internally eventually got the green light, I had already secured an offer in the commercial finance team at Kellogg's.

The actual needs that were going unmet for me were the pace I wanted to move at and the scope of opportunities to develop, as well as being pigeon-holed. The warning signs I picked up on to know that needs were going unmet were my energy, the effort it took to get things done and, of course, the enthusiasm for my work, which quickly diminished. In an effort to fix these myself, I looked elsewhere. For the record, I consider myself to be a much better general manager for having been an engineer first, with both a product manufacturing affinity and a problem-solving mindset helping me. Today, I call myself a right-brain engineer and a left-brain marketeer. So, don't be put off if you get pigeon-holed too; you can beat it.

Not all moves go like that. Many people stay and lose a lot of motivation putting up with a key need going unmet. Remaining in a situation that doesn't support you can be damaging in the long run.

> **Reflection – How are you feeling?**
> How do you feel about your current context? Are you engaged and motivated or frustrated? Can you identify what the problem is? Is something missing or do you have an unmet need?

Stress is a signal that things aren't right

Stress can often be an early warning sign that things are amiss. Many people talk about stressful situations in a generic way, but stressors are not the same for everyone. Many of the jobs that I choose to do are considered by other people to be highly stressful. For me, on the other hand, being active, busy, travelling a lot and having a challenge that stretches me are all things I thrive on. It's too much downtime, boredom, a lack of challenge or things like unfairness that cause me stress. However, although everyone has different pressure points, one very common thing that makes something a stressor is the amount of *choice* or *control* you have. Not having a choice can be frustrating, and when that builds to the point where you can't accept or stay on top of certain things, whatever the issue or topic, it is that 'internal frustration' that causes stress to rise.

Understanding what pushes your own buttons and causes mental or physical stress, and what that then looks like, will allow you to act sooner to change things. It could be an impact on your sleep habits, your energy levels, your general motivation or, indeed, your physical health. Many issues such as back problems, headaches and digestive problems can be associated with stress. Take note and see these as an indicator that things are not right.

Colleagues can provide the signal that things aren't right

Having colleagues you trust, or a strong and open relationship with your manager or mentor, will ensure you have people near you who are able to help you see things too. I was grateful in my very early years of being a mum when a colleague tapped me on the shoulder and asked me how I was. They let me know when I had been a little 'off hand' or curt in response to pressure from a new manager who was just finding his feet, and I was thus able to fix this instantly. Similarly, when I was a new managing director in the thick of union negotiations, I was able to adapt with a small nudge from my manager who saw my patience slipping and suggested I worked a few less hours in order to get more sleep and boost my energy. In each case, I regulated the situation or boosted my effectiveness with help from an outside voice to help me step back and gain more perspective.

How you react to change is a choice

Going through your career simply trying to avoid change is not very realistic. Accepting that change is a guaranteed fact of life is critical to managing your way through it. Recognising that something is wrong, out of sync or off balance is only the first part of the equation; taking steps to do something about it is critical. In the same way that you can choose what you prioritise or what to learn, it is your choice how to respond to change. Often, this will come down to the simplest choice – do you stay in the new changed context and adapt, or do you leave and find a better context?

Not all change comes in a big, defining moment of course; some things happen gradually. Spotting this type of subtle change and its impact on your outlook is less easy. Larger changes grab our attention and we adapt or act to adjust in response, but small changes in our environment and work which creep up on us can be detrimental if they go unacknowledged. Constant monitoring and being in tune with your environment makes it easier to spot when something may be gradually shifting in your context. I like to ask myself, every single week, in any job I'm in: Do I want to go to work this week? Do I like what I'm doing? Am I still in the right job and with the right company? Essentially, in this way, I *choose* to be in that situation, week in, week out. When the answer to any of those questions is either 'no' or 'I'm not sure', then I am able to look at why and take action accordingly.

Ask yourself the following and see where you are at. Figure 3.2 shows a list of questions that help highlight issues. This list is not exhaustive, and you might have other questions you want to regularly ask yourself, but it is a good place to start.

There's one key principle in data analysis: it's the pattern *over time* that is important, not simply the absolute number. One off day may not mean anything at all, but it's the trends you want to keep an eye on. To work out how much of an issue you have, ask these questions again after a few weeks or a month and see if the answers are clearer or if they have changed. You can answer 'yes' or 'no' or give a mark out of 10, it is up to you. What is important is to note any change.

Let's return to our cheetah. She is constantly assessing her situation, and she needs to adjust her skills, time her movements, be aware of the risks in her situation and think rapidly about how to position herself to best achieve the task at hand. For her, the cost of not paying attention to even the smallest nuances can mean the difference between survival and death. The cheetah takes her awareness of her skills and the confidence of knowing she's done this before and combines it with reading the situation, continuously. When the situation doesn't play to that combination of strengths and awareness, she moves on to find a new opportunity.

FIGURE 3.2: QUESTIONS TO CHECK IN ON YOUR FEELINGS, FRUSTRATIONS AND FULFILMENT OVER TIME.

	TIME 1	TIME 2	TIME 3
Are you happy?			
Are you motivated?			
Would you miss work if you didn't go back?			
Do you like what you do?			
Do you get on with your colleagues?			
Are you proud to work for the company?			
Do you feel valued?			
Do you get recognition for your work?			
Do you feel included?			
Can you be yourself?			
Are you fulfilled with this work?			
Are you progressing as expected?			
Is there something missing?			
Are you in control of your work?			
Are you bored?			

Once you can clearly see the context that you are in, as well as acknowledging that both your product map and your self-belief are things that you control, it's very easy to see how the decision to move on is something that you can also easily be in control of. I am often asked how I was able to make so many moves in my career, as if moving jobs is unusual, difficult or not something to be attempted that often. I don't consider myself to have moved an unusual amount, nor do I feel that it was necessarily hard. Not all the changes I made were prompted by my own choices, admittedly, but many were proactive, and in all cases I owned a great deal of the process and the making of the opportunities. Each move, regardless of initiative, was the result of something having changed in my current context.

There are different sources of change that come along, some of which will need more drastic action than others, and so recognising the driver for the change is the first step in deciding if you should deal with it and, if so, how. Not all changes need to result in a move. Some can be managed with adjustments in role and a refinement of your needs.

Over time, as you answer the questions from figure 3.2, this should give you an indication of where to look. In connecting it to the needs list in figure 3.1, you will narrow down what is missing. As you begin to observe when and how changes impact how you are performing, how productive you are and how happy you are, in life and in your career, you will have greater control over your destiny. You will be able to adapt.

4

Adaptability – The Future-Proof Skill

ADAPTABILITY IS your ability to deal with and thrive on change, whether that means being able to accommodate it within your current situation or being able to move to a new context. Adaptability, in my view, is a critical skill for the future. If you don't learn how to adapt, you will limit your effectiveness in your career, missing opportunities and falling behind, and maybe even becoming obsolete.

Some changes are thrown at you and others can be of your own causing, as a consequence of pursuing your goals or being less willing to accept the status quo, for example. That is what the cheetah metaphor is all about. Recognising the source of change and being able to adapt and move towards action, rather than being a passive victim of circumstance, is the essence of adaptability. All change can be conquered; the question is, how best to do it?

The two mirrors and the cheetah in harmony

What happens when we put the two mirrors and the cheetah together? This is when your self-awareness, your self-belief and your context are all supporting you, and you can thrive by being who you are. When change happens, the status quo is upset, but such is the relationship between knowing yourself, being yourself and understanding your context, that you only require an adaptation in one of the three areas to bring things back into harmony again. It can be your choice which element that is. Adaptation is like the 'glue' that links the two mirrors and the cheetah together.

The question to ask is: what do you adapt? Do you change your toolkit, learn a new skill, flex how you do things and modify some of the pieces that we looked at under self-awareness? Do you try and adapt what's important by changing your priorities or goals and what you stand for, in order to fit the change? Or is the change such that you are unwilling or unable to change things about yourself, your skills, your approach or your values, to such an extent that you need to move to a new context? Let's look at the levels of adaptation, one by one, and the types of changes that might arise.

Adapting your capabilities or product map

Making changes to your product map – in particular, to your toolkit – is far easier and less risky than other options. This is an approach that works well when accommodating small changes. Some examples of how people accommodate small changes are: learning new skills, taking on new industry standards or company policies and integrating with new teammates. Things that happen in the run of everyday work may require you to learn new skills, build new relationships or remember new steps. These changes require effort to accommodate, but for the majority of people, it should not feel that uncomfortable or insurmountable. You can ascertain how well you deal with run of the mill changes like this by checking in with yourself on how you feel. You can also seek feedback from colleagues, mentors or your manager.

Adapting priorities, values or goals

Though the idea of changing your values or goals may sound like you are hiding who you are as a person, it is actually a natural thing that happens as we grow. Making adjustments to your motivators or style may require a different trade-off or a new perspective and is often done in response to a major change such as life events, having children, caring for relatives or major sickness. Work-based examples might be a change of manager, a company restructure or a promotion. Larger changes like these will require a rethink of how you work and may have a bigger impact on your routine. Some might require you to reorganise how you operate or introduce many smaller changes all in one go, creating a steep learning curve. Particularly when of your own creation, these can be reason enough for you to change your priorities or even what you value. The challenge here is to give yourself room to make the necessary changes in habit; patience is key. Make sure that, in seeking to adapt your motivators or style, you don't go too far and end up hiding who you are. Changes in values and priorities are a natural part of life, but forcing a false change on yourself won't work. No longer being yourself, while this may work in the short term as an adaptation to change, is clearly not the idea.

Adapting your context

Moving jobs or making a career move is a less easy path, one that many people shy away from and avoid at all costs. But, sometimes it's needed for you to feel content. Such moves can be driven by many small changes or a large change that you cannot or will not accommodate. Some examples are: a lack of development opportunities, continuous skillset or job scope changes that don't interest you, being underappreciated, a lack of recognition and unfair treatment (whether perceived or actual). Consider, too, company strategy, policy or culture changes that may not resonate with you. These changes may make you feel a loss of motivation and enjoyment, or a rising frustration, all of which will tip the scales in favour of a braver move. We will cover ways to manage these scenarios in the next chapters.

There can be times when a context change for you is able to be fixed without the upheaval of a move, so long as the trade-off works for you. You may be willing to work on a project without a team for a short period, even though leadership is a need you have highlighted. Alternatively, you may find your activities are redrawn as the result of either a restructure or a change in systems and technology towards automation. Though not a move you may have been looking for, the resulting role could still fit your needs at least for a while.

Adapt or move?

When changes happen that upset your needs in such a way that it either takes a long time to correct or you can't see a way to correct it at all, then moving may become the necessary course of action. Key to recognising what kind of adaptation is best for you in any given circumstance lies in a fairly simple comparison: how much effort will it take for you to continue versus how much effort will be involved in a complete move. Again, as you perfect the art of self-awareness – particularly the understanding of where you get energy from and where your stressors lie – it will be easier for you to read these situations.

Some changes will be caused or initiated by your employer and your work situation, other changes will be initiated by you and your life situation, and yet others may simply arise naturally as you progress and grow in your career. A framework of questions can help you identify the sources of change and whether you can and want to adapt. Figure 4.1 shows the quick checklist of needs from Chapter 4 broken down into three categories: job, manager and company. Use the check box to note if change has happened in a big or small way, and which party initiated it.

FIGURE 4.1: SPOTTING CHANGES AND ADAPTATION

Needs	Was there a change?	Who initiated it?	Can you adapt?	Do you want to adapt?
JOB	YES/NO	YOU/ EMPLOYER	YES/NO	YES/NO
Scope				
Compensation				
Responsibility				
MANAGER				
Autonomy				
Recognition				
Feedback				
COMPANY				
Location				
Working hours				
Office layout				

As you track where change comes from alongside your desire to adapt to it, you begin to build a picture of how in control of your career you are. Asking yourself whether you can adapt, and then whether you want to, is a good way of addressing a problem and laying it to rest with an action you can accept. Alternatively, you can simply log the thing as a future limitation and accept it in such a way that the frustration does not build unnecessarily. In other words, you can decide that, although the change is undesirable, you can live with it for now. The more this kind of undesirable-but-acceptable change happens, the easier it becomes to decide to move.

In one of the mergers I went through, the resulting culture, which was a change driven by the company, meant a very different way of working. I went from relatively informal meetings and report writing to extreme structure, task management and a reduction in local business unit responsibility; these were changes I did not like. I chose not to adapt and sought a new role. Needless to say, however, I adapted for the short term while I was still employed there.

At other times, I have experienced changes to the teams that I manage as part of a restructure. This is quite common. The essence of the job remains the same, but the reporting lines can change and 'pieces' of your team can be removed or added. This can sometimes mean a change in manager. If you are playing the long game with an employer, then these types of change will require adaptation and trust. If you are not deeply vested in your future at this specific company, then that amount of change may be enough for you to look elsewhere.

> **Reflection – Movement is becoming more common**
> The world is shaping for portability, flexibility and continuous movement, regardless of the driver of the changes (technology, sustainability, etc.) So, it's realistic to expect that, at some point, whether you've done so in the past or just considered it, you too will move between employers or between teams or departments. Can you see that happening? Will you be ready?

Employment is a two-way street

Of course, it is important to recognise that you are not the only one with needs. Companies have their needs too. When both of those sets of needs are aligned, everything is set to grow in harmony. When both sets of needs are out of alignment, however, the relationship can be in jeopardy and a parting of ways is likely. Often, we think of instances such as a restructure or a cost-cutting exercise that results in job losses, but it can be something as simple as the company moving to a location you don't want to commute or relocate to. That situation quite clearly points to a resolution with the two sides parting company. Alternatively, there's the common occurrence of a change in family structure (a new child, an older family member coming into the household or a new disability to manage, etc.), leading to someone wanting to work more flexibly with reduced hours or on a different timeframe to fit the role of carer. While that request is increasingly more common and able to be met, it is still not widely available from all employers as they may have needs that don't accommodate that option just yet. This situation, too, could lead to a parting of the ways. There are also, of course, the less amicable situations where behaviour crosses a line and an employer's threshold requirements are not met. Finally, and perhaps most importantly, there are the various combinations of partial needs being met on both sides i.e. situations that exist between those two 'edge' scenarios. The most common scenario is probably where one side's needs are unmet, and that is where adjustment and effort come into consideration. With a little work on both sides, the situation could be resolved.

I find it helpful to think of employment as a two-way street. Remember, wherever a change originates, the adaptation should not always need to come from you. Adjustment and effort to accommodate change can come from your employer too. I have met many people who assume something won't be available or granted by an employer or manager, when they have not even asked. But companies invest in talent, and avoiding unnecessary attrition is important to them. Just as you will need to decide whether it is more effort to move jobs or to put up with undesired changes, your company will have to decide between losing a valuable employee and searching for a replacement, onboarding them and so on, or simply making some perhaps inconvenient changes that will make their current employee happy to stay.

Make it a first step to try and negotiate a change to your current context before giving up on it. You may be surprised. Flexible working is a perfect example of this. Before the 2020 COVID-19 pandemic made home working a necessity for many, I began to work from home one to two days a week, reaping the benefits of cutting out the one hour 40-minute commute and gaining more focus than the open-plan office set up at Amazon allowed me to have. I found this flexibility to be a great source of productivity and was surprised how few people chose to use the opportunity. When enquiring of colleagues why more people didn't use it, I frequently heard the answer that it would not be allowed by their manager or not deemed suitable for their team. Some genuinely believed it was a benefit for senior people that would be unlikely to be allowed for them. They may, of course, have been right in their suppositions, as each situation is different, but I found it astounding that these individuals had not actually asked!

I found the same scepticism to be true around the use of sabbaticals, something that Amazon offered in the countries I worked in. I heard some senior managers talk of them not being 'doable' at senior level, and that a sabbatical was perhaps more suitable for younger employees who classically head off backpacking in their late 20s. To put this myth to rest, I took a three-month sabbatical as a director, and it allowed me to focus on a personal issue. I had a need, and instead of stepping away from my job completely, which I didn't want to do, I found the company to be accommodating if I simply asked and planned accordingly.

Here's another example of how a good company can adapt to meet the needs of its employees. Around the time of the initial Brexit vote in 2016, I found myself living in Germany, an EU country that was not my nationality nor that of my husband, who is Dutch. Not knowing what the steps would be on UK departure from the EU, the one thing that was evident was that my husband and I were in a country that was not where we would both choose to retire. Should Brexit result in a choice to stay put or return 'home', we would have a problem. In this instance, rather than leave my job and look for one in the UK or the Netherlands, Amazon was open to a relocation. I moved country and did the same job, director of European beers, wines and spirits, from the UK. I did change manager as a result, but that was not a problem. My teams all kept me as their leader, and we were all able to adapt. This was a great level of adaptability on both sides, something I am grateful for. Imagine if neither side had checked; what a waste that would have been!

So, when you are facing change – big or small – the question of 'what next' depends on what adaptation is needed, what is feasible and by whom. Figure 4.2 shows a visual way of thinking about this.

The four quadrants in this matrix represent the adaptation scenarios for the combinations of needs being met or unmet, for both employer and employee. For example, in the bottom right, where change is initiated by you, a new need for you emerges or an existing one is not being met. The challenge for your employer is how much they can adapt to those new needs? This would be consistent with a new flexible working request, for example. In the top left quadrant, change comes from your employer, and the challenge is how much or how quickly you can adapt. Both these scenarios require effective communication to ensure awareness, feasibility and willingness to adapt. In the event of either a lack of willing or poor communication, needs can continue to go unmet. When left unresolved, this can lead to tension and disappointment.

FIGURE 4.2: NEEDS VERSUS ADAPTATION

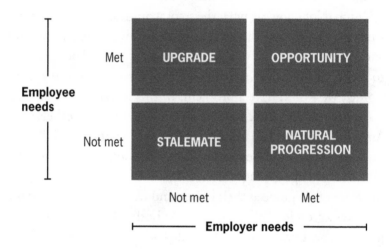

Let's now take a closer look at these four types of adaptation scenarios, some tips on handling them, and any resulting moves that arise when adaptation is not possible.

Opportunity

This is a great box to be in. Opportunities come to you unsolicited. It is not uncommon for this to happen while needs are still being met, for both you and your employer. People know what type of things you can reliably deliver. You are appearing on people's radars, and it's a good thing. Opportunities find you from outside the company, or from within your current organisation, as your reputation precedes you.

Finding yourself in this box is the result of delivering a strong performance, combined with communicating and setting future expectations, whether that be for your career path internally, or showcasing your work externally, via social media or advocates you have created along the way. In this situation, new opportunities arrive before you exhaust the learning in your current position, and so you avoid the challenge of being unfulfilled as a result of outgrowing your role.

This is, in some ways, the ideal situation, and it is what my manager at Nike all those years ago had hinted at: that my brand would drive demand for me and my talent by bringing opportunities to my door, instead of me having to fight to find them. This is a plus, so long as you have cultivated a reputation for the things you want to do and be known for. If that's the case, the opportunities landing at your door will appeal to you.

If you find yourself in the situation where you frequently get opportunities but, all too often, you don't like them or they lack something you would be looking for, perhaps your communication or 'marketing' of yourself needs adapting? A reflection back to the self-awareness section could help correct this.

Natural career progression

In this box, when your needs are not being met, you become dissatisfied or unfulfilled in one way or another and seek out an adaptation from your employer or manager. If this isn't possible, it will likely result in a move. I called this box 'natural progression' because learning follows a pattern and people move on. In each role, over time, an individual will progress through phases. They struggle, initially, as they get to grips with a new area and the learning curve is steep. They then start to perform as the learning curve softens. They then over-perform as the learning curve plateaus, and as they run out of challenges, it is only natural to seek the next opportunity for development. If you are performing well, you will likely reach a point of unmet needs before your employer does. Essentially, this could be small things which don't leave you as satisfied, a lack of challenge as you gain mastery in your role, for example, but which still leave a satisfying situation for your employer as you are performing well. At this juncture, the first port of call would be with your manager and your current company to address those needs. Oftentimes, new opportunities or changes to your role or context will be possible, and other times it requires action from you to close that needs gap.

This is one of two boxes where a move does not necessarily need to be to a new company, and where open communication, honesty and setting expectations can help you and your employer create an opportunity together. If that doesn't work, then you would begin hunting elsewhere and move on 'naturally' and, hopefully, amicably.

Upgrade

When adaptation is required and you fail to acknowledge it, there may be consequences that you don't see coming. In this box, your needs are being met and you might even be coasting, but your employer's needs can go unmet. If the need is either a new skill set, a physical presence in a new location or a need for you to travel, there are ways around this if you can adapt.

Where the employer's needs continue to go unmet because they lie in areas you are unaware of or are unwilling to recognise, this is a dangerous blind spot. If left unaddressed, this situation can lead to a point of no return and result in you being made redundant or let go. Again, self-awareness of your styles and behaviours should help you avoid such situations. Ensuring you have avenues for communication and feedback with your manager (and peers, where relevant) can prepare you to ease the situation or avoid it altogether.

Stalemate

Sometimes, things don't align and both sides see it is over. This is a more unusual situation, where neither the employee's nor the employer's needs are being met. Take, for example, a major restructure, where someone's existing role does not exist and substitute roles do not appeal to them or are not feasible for them to carry out. Amicable separation is often the solution here.

On the other end of the spectrum, where small changes lead to dissatisfaction for an employee whose needs become more difficult to meet and dissatisfaction for the employer for whom the resulting performance is also becoming less satisfying, we have a problem. In this situation, an exit looks likely, but both parties are not in agreement or able to acknowledge the situation, and this often leads to a more negative process. An example of this could be where employees have displayed unacceptable or undesirable behaviour. If the employee is not open to changing, the employer may initiate a move. Finding yourself in this situation is likely to be the result of poor self-awareness: not seeing, hearing or being able to digest and appreciate the feedback that would precede such a serious situation.

Getting comfortable with the fact that all four types of scenario exist will make it easier to be prepared. Recognising the needs of either side will help you adapt, either in role or by moving on. It is imperative to reflect in order to proceed appropriately without being too hasty.

By understanding your most important needs – those that make up your ideal context – you will be able to make more confident decisions about the more difficult career moves. When looking for adaptation from your employer and from yourself, keep in mind your non-negotiable or walk-away scenario, to know when you are at a dead end.

For me, that measure is ensuring my drive or my internal fire stays alive. The day I can't be bothered, don't feel I am making a difference, don't feel valued or lose my passion for the job in front of me, is the day I look to change. Do you know what that measure might be for you? You will often find that it is connected to your values and where you get your energy. Expressing this as a need and including it in your 'must have' needs list will ensure that, in the event you do move on, you will still come away from the experience having learnt something important, and you'll make sure that need is met in the next role you seek.

Stop – Breathe – Think – Act

A hobby of mine, before I had kids, was scuba diving. I can remember very clearly the mantra for dealing with emergency or panic situations: Stop – Breathe – Think – Act. When something happens underwater, and when air supply is limited and critical, taking time to slow to a stop and ensure you are breathing well and calmly is always the first step. This is followed by a measured consideration before any action is taken, simply because there is no scope for getting it wrong.

I now use the same phrase in coaching my teams to deliver effective and clear presentations, something I learnt right at the start of my career. People often avoid public speaking as they fear they will forget what they want to say, go blank and be stuck, mute in front of an audience. The challenge is to invite the pregnant pause in, to simply learn to 'be'; to stand in front of an audience with no words, rather than stumble continuously with little clarity. The power of standing still, slowing to observe the situation and taking a breath is of huge value in registering what's going on and using that perspective to decide what to do next. For diving, clearly safety is the primary concern, and running out of breath is an actual possibility. For presentations, overcoming the fear of not knowing what to say, or actively using a pause to think before speaking, is a very effective way of not running out of control.

The same approach can be applied to your career moves, regardless of how you arrive at that metaphorical crossroads. Stop –Breath – Think – Act. Having found yourself in the midst of a move, it makes sense to take stock. This is such a pivotal moment that there is always lots to learn, even if only to confirm that the steps you are taking align with your plan. More so, because the situation gives you an opportunity to learn, to understand and also to check that you know *why* you are moving and that you are moving *towards* something as opposed to running away.

If we reflect again on our cheetah, who moved into a new situation driven by her precision thinking and her ability to draw on her own energy and skills, her course of action would very likely be different if she were running towards a hunting situation in search of new prey, fuelled by a full belly, as opposed to running away from an attack that went badly, resulting in no kill, exhaustion or even injuries.

When making a career move, if you are leaving because you are dissatisfied or because you didn't want to adapt to the role's requirements, then it's important to address these problems before you take the leap rather than just run away from them. Otherwise, you could run the risk of repeating the same situation in your next role.

Had I done that between some of the earlier moves I made in the first 10 years of my career, I may have learnt more. Who knows? Certainly, if everything had been plain sailing, I may not have had the wake-up calls that I shared at the beginning of this book, which suggests I was running from situation to situation without fully learning in between. The insight you gain in reflecting on why and how you have arrived at the point of making a move is invaluable.

Here's an example. Around the age of 29, I was applying to business school to study an MBA, something I had always planned to do. As I considered what I might do if I was unsuccessful, I flipped a coin. Heads, I would change tack and lean into my diving hobby by qualifying as a diving instructor. Tails, I would stick with a more 'traditional' career path and try for another MBA programme somewhere else. As it happened, my application was eventually successful so the coin toss became moot, but there was a point when it looked like it would be all too relevant. Although I was accepted to the school, there was a moment of doubt. The well-established French campus sent me a rejection letter a couple of weeks before the newly-founded Singapore campus called with an offer. So, for those few weeks, I was facing down my impulsive decision-making and contemplating restarting a new life under the sea! Rather than jumping for joy about the thought of life as a diving instructor, though, I grappled with accepting failure. I had succeeded at most things I had attempted up to that point, and this rejection hit hard.

The point of the story is this: after I got the call from Singapore, I could have brushed off those uncomfortable few weeks of rejection as simply nothing – after all, I got accepted to the MBA programme anyway! However, taking my own advice to Stop – Breathe – Think – Act forced me to actually reflect on why I felt so bad about the rejection. Instead of merely worrying about the technicalities of what my next steps would be, I was able to really think about what mattered to me and to take the chance to grow from the experience. Imagine if I had simply rushed ahead with my scuba diving plan. Not only would I have missed out on the invaluable reflection I gained from the initial rejection, but I might have actually missed out on the opportunity in Singapore, which was amazing and one where I made life-long friends!

Stand still every now and then. Think before you leap. Is your logic sound? Even when it is a positive move, the confirmation that you are sticking to your plan and grasping a great opportunity is very reassuring and a boost in itself. Alternatively, when it's not such a positive move, you have the chance to refocus and learn how not to repeat any mistakes or lost opportunities in your next step. If, like I did, you hit a bump and have failed at something along the way, try to understand it so you can overcome it and learn. Remember, failure is our friend! Inventors build in failure as the most statistically likely outcome. Treat setbacks as one of the possible outcomes as you craft who you are and innovate in your career path. All moves are valid.

Process the departure

Step one in any plan to move on to new opportunities has to start with understanding, accepting and processing the actual departure from your current job. That might seem rather obvious. Equally it might not even seem relevant, depending on how you have made moves up until this point. In situations where the individual chooses to resign, move on and accept a new job, it's reasonably straightforward. The moment of accepting that a move is necessary has often come far in advance of the actual move itself. These are the easiest moves to make because, from the first moment, the individual is in the driving seat, actively looking for and securing the next opportunity. In other situations, where the choice to move does not come from the individual themselves, then the acknowledgement of a move occurs very close to the departure itself. If you or your role are being restructured or you are being fired, then there is often a moment of denial that the situation is happening. Until that has been processed emotionally, it is very difficult, in fact almost impossible, to move on positively and coherently in search of the next opportunity.

Why does this matter? Take our cheetah. If she doesn't succeed in securing her prey and killing the gazelle which she was chasing, then either she and her offspring are left with no food, or worse still, she gets injured in that encounter. Step one must be recovering from her wound, otherwise she will not be in the best position to continue to hunt and she may harm herself even further. In work situations, where the move or exit has not been something that you were in control of, take time to understand and process it. Try to take responsibility for the circumstances around how your employment came to an end. You need to let the wound of separation heal well. If you fail to do this, then you are probably going to be less able to convincingly portray a strong character to the next recruiter, and that can harm your chances of securing your next role.

So, stop, even if only briefly, to reflect and breathe. Use this time as a re-energising and refocusing moment, and then move forward, with purpose, to act. In this way, you will make the right move happen.

> **Reflection – Past moves**
> Looking at the moves you have made in your career to date, do you understand what caused you to seek change? Did you fix the missing 'need' in the move, or did you find it re-emerged? What would you do differently in your next move?

PART 2

APPLYING THE KNOWLEDGE

5

The Job Hunt

Throughout this second part of the book, we will look at how to take what you have learned from the two mirrors and the cheetah and use it to help you navigate your career in practice, to create a more fulfilling set of experiences. The initial chapters focus on you as an individual and your own career path, making deliberate moves and dealing with various career situations. Each one of these is broken down into clear and detailed steps, though, so don't panic! Changing jobs can be daunting, but we're going to take it one step at a time. After this, we will look at how the two mirrors and the cheetah can be used to support people who report to you, and then how to think about incorporating the model into a reflective, healthy rhythm over time. For now, though, let's focus on the big topic of making a job change, which may or may not result in a significant career change.

Changing jobs is not unusual, and the data now suggests that the average person will do so five to seven times over their career. This number increases the younger you are, as future generations gear up for a far more flexible approach to life. Nonetheless, it's not something we go through every day, which means it is unlikely to be second nature for most people and, understandably, can involve some level of trepidation.

Personally, I have experienced everything from changes to the scope of my role to crafting a complete career move, so I have perhaps had more than my fair share of adaptation to context changes. This affords me the luxury of experience, and it has allowed me to see patterns which emerge in many of those situations. I have experienced the range of 'exit doors': resignations which were sometimes smooth, sometimes too quick; perfectly-timed promotions; planned development moves and also being restructured out of a job; and yes, I've been 'exited' too. Though not often talked about, you'll be surprised how common the latter is, and as unsettling as it might sound, if it happens to you, don't worry. It doesn't mean it's the end of your career. It just means that job was not the right fit for you, for whatever reason. Try to use your self-awareness to learn from the situation and make better moves for yourself going forward.

Whether you are considering a move, have taken the decision to move on already or you've found yourself 'moved', you are in a period of transition. Managing that transition, from the start of the thought process and through all the interactions that follow, is a key part of your career. And, sometimes, it can have a larger impact on your reputation than your actual performance in a role, so it is worthwhile doing it right.

To hunt is to seek, to pursue and to capture. To search is to seek something carefully and thoroughly. Two concepts which are similar but not identical. I choose to refer to the process as a job hunt, so there is clarity on the need to actively capture the opportunity once you have found it. Put simply, it is not just what you do but how you do it. Remember that *you* are your secret weapon. Use it well.

The process of job hunting, when done well, is so much more

than just the CV, the job advert and the interview. Approaching it with a fresh mindset, and the wider knowledge of yourself gained in Part 1 of this book, will allow you to own the process and take greater control. Let's take a look, one by one, at the steps you can take to achieve this.

Step 1: Get out of neutral and into gear

The job hunt process can take a lot of energy, so in addition to getting organised, starting with the right frame of mind is imperative. Competition for jobs is fierce, so having only one foot in the water, casually looking but not actively going for it, will show through and is not likely to cut it. There needs to be a moment where you commit to the process and get your mind into gear. Think of it this way: when your car is in neutral, although you can coast or glide, you cannot drive your vehicle. It is essentially out of control for that moment, which leaves you helpless as you turn a corner, unaware of what is waiting for you. Equally, if you are not in gear when you get into your job hunt, you aren't driving so you are less able to be proactive or take compelling action, making it harder to rise above the competition waiting around the corner or to respond to opportunities.

Commitment and drive can be as compelling to hiring managers and recruiters as other skills and qualities, so don't underestimate it. You are the product and you need to make a sale. The best salesperson I ever met was at 10-year-old boy on the streets in Cambodia. The last thing I needed was a book. I bought a book. I know plenty of people who give in to sales tactics simply to move on and get away from such pressure sellers, but I have never had a problem with saying a firm 'no, thank you'.

The boy approached my husband and I as we were on the outskirts of Siem Reap, having visited the famous Angkor Wat site. We were not the only tourists at that spot, and this young boy flitted from person to person with a couple of paperback books under his arm. When he approached us, the first thing he asked was where we came from, suggesting the UK. I told him I *was*, and he immediately became very animated and started asking which football clubs we supported, talking about David Beckham and other famous players. When he asked my husband who his favourite player was, he mentioned that he wasn't from the UK himself, but from the Netherlands.

Immediately, this boy pivoted to an equally impressive set of statistics and popular stories from the Netherlands, starting with Ajax, the football team which my husband supports. This carried on despite me declining to buy a book a few times, and all the while we were choosing somewhere to have lunch as the boy worked tirelessly and very happily in sharing facts, asking questions and building a relationship.

As we sat in the very open street restaurant, devouring the most addictively tasty and spicy Khmer curries, he spotted us. He came back directly to us about half an hour later, carrying with him not only his original books, but some written in Dutch. The tenacity and creativity he demonstrated in finding a common wavelength to connect on, and the research he must have undertaken to be able to do that for any different type of nationality, was simply astounding. I began to like this little boy the more he spent time with us, albeit uninvited at the side of our restaurant table. Impressed by the effort he had put in, I took interest in his small selection of books and ended up purchasing *The Khmer Rouge*, a local history that allowed me to learn about the place we were visiting.

To be clear, had the boy simply followed us, with a repetitive narrative and a pushy insistence on making a sale, then I would have felt this was just harassment, and I certainly wouldn't have given in and bought a book. The reason I was happy to change

my mind and consider a purchase was because of the commitment
and the energy this boy showed in understanding his customers,
in building a relationship and in knowing exactly what he had to
sell to us tourists. His unwavering commitment to making a sale
was truly endearing, and as it turned out, he did have something
that interested me and added an extra dimension to my time in
Cambodia. If I can only muster half of that commitment every
time I seek to influence and make a sale, I will be happy!

As you go into your job hunt, your commitment or lack of
it will come through whether you recognise it or not, and with
such competition in tough times this is an area in which you can
shine. So, get out of neutral, get into gear and drive the process
actively. Demonstrate to recruiters just how much you want it.

Step 2: Define what success looks like

A simple and yet very often overlooked first question is: do you
know what you are looking for? One of Stephen Covey's *The 7
Habits of Highly Effective People*[8] is: 'Begin with an end in mind.'
(This book is well worth a read if you haven't yet encountered it!)
Job hunting is a project of great importance, so giving it emphasis and planning it with a vision is completely appropriate. Fast
forward to the end of the process and ask yourself: what is your
desired result? In simple terms, I guess you want to have found
a job with a context that fulfils your needs and where you will
thrive. Take time to visualise what things will look like when you
have found that ideal role. Be as specific with yourself as you can
in defining what you are looking for externally, using as many of
the elements of your product map as possible and your needs as
they relate to a full definition of your desired context. Are you
able to describe the shortcomings of your current or previous
positions and therefore the things which you are specifically *not*

looking for? It's good practice to note these down too so as to avoid the past repeating itself.

Returning to the tasks in both mirrors and the cheetah, armed with the knowledge of how to be yourself, what your needs are and how to navigate context, will you be able to recognise when an opportunity offers what you need to thrive? There will always be occasions where employment is simply needed as a means of paying the bills or when other things take priority; when it doesn't matter quite so much what the wider picture is. However, as you look to develop your career, money alone is unlikely to satisfy all your needs, so it's recognising those needs beyond the pay cheque that are the focus here.

List your 'ideal' needs

Surprising as it might be, a step often omitted from the job hunt is the target. You can build a list of must-have and nice-to-have criteria on which to rate opportunities that you consider. Include skills you want to use, values to be met, alignment with your goals and elements of the environment (think back to your context needs from job, manager and company in figure 3.1 in Part 1). List these criteria and rank them in order of importance. This will help you to avoid securing a role only to realise at the end of the process that a key element will not be met. If an obvious ranking is not easy to arrive at when looking at the list as a whole, then prioritise each to eventually surface the top critical few.

Frame your window of time

Motivate yourself into action by setting a due date. One of my favourite sayings is: 'The difference between a dream and a goal is a deadline.' Making something happen often requires you to visualise the end result too, so be specific about when you aim to land your new gig. It's not so much about the precise date you want to achieve it by. Rather, by setting a date, you ensure you don't fall foul of the procrastination monster. If you need the next job to have continuity in paying the bills because you already moved on, then this should not be a big issue, as your funds will dictate the patience you have. If, however, you've decided to move on in order to change a poor situation, but you've not yet let go of your current employment, it can be all too easy to slip back into habit and let the potential anxiety of the job hunt process stop you from actually following through. So, set your expectations on a certain timeframe to force the matter. You may choose to tell a close confidant about it too, to give yourself accountability.

Step 3: Showcase what you bring and sell it!

Remember that employment is a two-way street. You are stepping into a job marketplace, and as in any marketplace, it is one matching buyers with sellers. Yes, you need to 'window shop' the job opportunities that are available, checking out those with your broad criteria, but you also have to sell yourself. Just like market traders, you need to present your product in the best way. Although just a small shift in mindset, this will help you target specifically where to look and match what you have to offer with what people want to 'buy'. Using that mindset, think about how you can best sell yourself and how you ensure you stand out. Do you know what your USP (unique selling point) is? It is there in your product map from Chapter 1.

Let's use the analogy of consumer products. Would you buy any complex product if the details of what it was, how it worked and where it was from were not clearly articulated on the packaging? There are a few people I know, like those that bid for unopened luggage at airport auctions, who just can't resist the element of surprise and are not easily disappointed, for whom the answer to that question is 'yes'. But most of us wouldn't. You, as the product, need some detail behind you.

Leverage and connect all your materials

Consider carefully your CV/resume, your cover letters, your communications and all the material that reflects on you. These are your packaging; they are your marketing materials and your advertising campaign. Your digital footprint counts too, so whether it is a personal website, LinkedIn profile, Facebook, Twitter or Instagram account, make sure your online presence is consistent with the rest, including content you write and comments you make on others' posts. Whether you planned for it or not, recruiters, hiring managers and researchers can quite easily search for information on you in an astoundingly effective way. Social media, and your presence online, endures long after the initial post. Although you may not be able to change what is already out there, being aware of what people find when they look you up will at least leave you forewarned and in the best place to deal with it should it arise during the process. Look at all your material together and check that it communicates who you are, not a stereotype that lacks differentiation.

Answer the question: 'Why you?'

From the start of the process, you and your materials need to show why it should be you. Having specified what you are looking for, translate that backwards into elements that would contribute to such a role and environment. Does your CV say what you can bring? Does it describe how you can help an employer, and does it show how you have done this before? Do you read it and recognise yourself and your distinctive qualities? Or does it read as a list of job titles anyone could have held? A short profile summary is your chance to convey who you are. Bring together what you learnt about yourself in mirrors one and two in a few sentences. The one guaranteed thing that other candidates don't have in their armoury is your unique profile: the combination of skills, characteristics, passions, background and experiences that make you, you.

Invest time in carving out a punchy but accurate descriptor for yourself and help hiring managers get to know you. Dare to be different, but stay true to who you are. While there are many things that can be included in a CV, there is one thing that all recruiters and hiring managers will agree on: it should never contain false claims. Tempting though it may be to boost your chances with a few 'creative' claims about what you can do, it will only catch you out later down the line.

Demonstrate your value – be FAB

If you are looking for tips on exactly how to write your CV and what to put in there, you will find many different opinions depending on the type and level of roles you are thinking of. There is no doubt, however, that employers want to see what skills you bring, what experience you have, what education or training you've achieved and what interests you have. Keep it balanced, and remember the incredible diversity that you have without even trying. Having a life outside of work, and interests, is a relevant piece of information that shows a rounded individual, so don't skip it. Remember, however, that until you get in front of recruiters and win them over, you will need to entice, with firm evidence of past performance. You are fabulous. Not only is this the mindset you need to sell yourself with conviction, it can be shortened to FAB, a handy acronym I use to make sure I am sharing the most persuasive information which stands for feature, amount and benefit. This will help you to break down your achievements. What exactly was it you did? Make sure you fully describe the *feature*. How much of that thing was there? Quantify it with some dimensions by giving what you're talking about a concrete *amount*. Finally, remember to describe what it brought to your previous employer: how did you bring *benefit* to the organisation?

Step 4: Get your story straight

From the layout of your CV, to the structure and rationale of your covering letter or initial communications, to the first conversation and (hopefully) subsequent interviews, it pays to get your story straight. I'm not suggesting for one minute that you embellish your background and journey; it is, after all, your past and can't be changed. However, although the elements that make up your story may not change, the way you tell that story can. The point here is that it is *your* story to tell. Own it, and do not be ashamed of it. Think of common questions that may jump out to your prospective CV readers. It makes sense to tackle the answers to these while you're in the phase of creating your materials. This ensures that, in conversations and interviews, it creates a natural and cohesive picture that you are comfortable talking about, as opposed to something that catches you off guard or that you feel you have to explain as a defect.

Explain your motivation for moving

Having used the model of the two mirrors and the cheetah, it should be very easy for you to understand your motivation to move jobs and to articulate convincingly both what you are look-ing for and why. As a hiring manager, I want to see you on fire at the chance to work at the company and in my team. When you know *why* you want something, let it show. It is a powerful show of confidence to know where you're going and why, and it shows you've done your homework. This is even true of situations where you are moving from an environment that was not supporting your needs. It will show an interviewer that you possess enough self-awareness to have recognised that and taken steps to change it, which is of huge credit to you. As long as the emphasis is on what you're looking for that you didn't have before, rather than criticising other companies or managers, recruiters will understand, so don't feel you have to cover up the truth.

The whys and hows of past moves

A big piece of getting to know a candidate it is not only understanding what they've done, but why they chose to do it and why things came to an end. This information is useful as they can gain insight into how you may view opportunities and your potential longevity in their organisation. If you have an exit from an employer on your CV where a role came to an abrupt or unplanned end, it can be difficult to talk about initially. I have seen this struggle in a number of individuals whom I have mentored over the years, and I did too, the first time it happened to me. But this is a common situation; companies and individuals part ways all the time. Restructuring certainly happens frequently, as companies continually have to manage costs, and at the time of writing, the COVID-19 pandemic has put many more people in this situation of an abrupt end to their employment.

It's very important not to waste energy worrying about what cannot be changed. Instead, learn to talk about it in a way that is not damaging to either party. It's important, too, that you don't lose yourself down a rabbit hole of giving a full, blow-by-blow account of any situations or the differences that gave rise to the departure. Remember mirror two: you are no less valuable and no less confident just because somebody tells you so. The exit that happened to you does not change how good you are, nor should an uncomfortable question in an interview about that situation change your belief in yourself – be prepared, and stand firm.

If you have been uncomfortable about one of your departures, it can help to practise talking about it a number of times, and in different ways, to find an approach that you feel is honest and shows reflection. This can help you put that moment in time aside emotionally and move on as a stronger individual. The same practice can work if you have raced out of jobs and jumped around. Piecing it together with a rationale helps you take control of that story. For the first eight years of my career, I did two years per job and per company. Was I an impatient, non-committed individual, lacking stamina? Or was I a focused individual, willing to change to maintain pace in pursuing a career with ambition? To me, my behaviour was an example of trialling different roles and building a toolkit of skills from various vantage points in the chain, on my route to general management. All of the roles were connected by a common thread of the consumer products industry. Try and create your rationale for moments in your CV that you are less certain of, and fit them to your storyline.

'Sell' the gap in your employment

What's the problem with a gap in your employment history? This has to be the most agonised-over point that I come across when delivering career development sessions. Personally, I don't see the issue and I don't have a problem with it; and, yes, I've had a gap. It's important to note that there are very different definitions of what constitutes a gap. Is this time out to have children, is it a year between college and university or between education and full-time employment, or is it a mid-career sabbatical? It really doesn't matter. For the record, not all recruiters think about this as irrelevant, but bear with me. As a hiring manager myself, I would like to challenge you to think of it differently and hold onto it proudly.

When I first worked in the Netherlands, I was interviewing people for an entry-level position, and in reviewing CVs with other international colleagues, the topic of the 'year out' emerged. The insight I gained, sitting in that environment, was that it was considered a shortcoming of a candidate if they *hadn't* had a year out, as the general consensus was that a year of life experience is something not to be missed out on.

I have, over the years, packed in a number of backpacking trips, a sabbatical for a family health issue and some admittedly short maternity leaves. Although these weren't large periods of time, from taking these 'absences from the workforce' (for want of a better description) I can really see the value that can be gained in an alternative way to having simply continued in employment.

Who is to say that the learning of an individual who takes a year to go backpacking or surfing off the coast of Australia at an early age would be any less than one remaining in a dead-end job and losing motivation? I choose this example as it is the most stereotypical idea of what happens on a year out, often held by those who are not in favour of the 'gap year'; but of course, a year away could be used for almost anything. How about the individual who goes to Africa to help local farmers build an irrigation system? Or even the person forced to take leave to deal with a major illness or to care for a family member? I guarantee you these individuals will return with far broader experience and new perspectives than those not doing it.

Making decisions on a risky mountainside, learning new languages and experiencing new cultures, or learning how precious life is when it can no longer be taken for granted are valuable things. So, choose carefully how you mention them, but please, please do not feel you need to hide them because they are a valid part of your story. Diverse perspectives come from all of your experiences, not just those that happen at work.

How you decide to talk about these experiences is your choice. The key is to remember that others may not value it as highly, at least initially, so your challenge is to show what that time brought to you, what perspectives you now have or what you have learned having done it. The tides are turning on valuing all of these perspectives without bias, but for the moment, there is still a 'sales' job to be done on promoting your non-work experience! Use it to your advantage.

Step 5: Widen your playing field as you explore

We have already covered the importance of knowing *what* you are looking for. Which type of industry are you looking to be in? Which type of function or department are you targeting? What size of company are you happier in? You will hopefully have asked yourself these questions as part of starting your job hunt.

You *could* take a fairly linear approach to answering these questions. By considering which jobs you have held in the past, or what your education has prepared you to focus on, you will derive a template and be able to approach similar roles. However, this may well be limiting you more than you realise. An alternative, more flexible approach, is to look at the *skills* you have, and see which ones are transferable. Look at all the types of skills you have, and look at what types of roles need those skills. The more you can be adaptable and open to learning, the wider you can cast your net for opportunities. Where are your skills needed?

Finance is an easy example of something transferable. You might work in the finance team on the general ledger in a computer software company. You could choose to target different types of finance roles within other computer software companies, or you could take your finance skills to the pharmaceutical industry. Your ability to adapt and to think differently is the way to unlock both of those avenues.

The tech industry is a perfect example of where the ability to learn and adapt is far more important than specific functional knowledge, at least for some of the non-software development roles. Certainly, in my time recruiting at Amazon, the focus on how people were able to work was as important, if not more so, than the industry which they came from or the roles they previously held. I went to Amazon with 25 or so years of experience in the consumer industry, but I had never worked in retail nor had I worked in tech. I had a certain work style and ability to lead which were desired at Amazon, but not the specific experience of the business I went in to run. I was willing to learn and Amazon was willing to let me. In my time at Amazon to date, I have spent five years in three completely different parts of the business, leveraging my adaptability and skills rather than my acquired experience alone.

Don't fixate on the job title

How many times have you looked at the title on a job description and wondered what it actually means? The creativity in naming of roles is endless and not always of help to the candidate. Job titles can be misleading, so don't get distracted by them – instead, look for opportunities in the marketplace based on the skills and the types of responsibilities they require and not simply on the names of those jobs.

Take the title of product manager. This is quite a simple name, and yet the skills required for a product manager working on a brand of toothpaste are worlds away from a product manager delivering on-demand video or a product manager in investment banking. Likewise, requirements for an operations manager in the restaurant business are likely to be very different to an operations manager in the gas and oil fields. The trick is to look for environments that can meet your needs, perhaps by investigating the cultures of companies, and then seeing how your skills could be used.

Look at which types of roles, industries or companies might have a need right now for the types of skills which you have and not necessarily those looking for the specific track record of experience that you bring. This will give you a fresh look and present opportunities that you might otherwise pass by.

Step 6: Hunt and create opportunities

If you have ever moved internally, been promoted or taken part in succession planning, it should be no surprise that not all job opportunities are posted externally. The risks, costs and timelines (usually) are far better for a company when appointing internal candidates, but it doesn't mean there isn't a better candidate externally. That could be you. The advantages of having an out-sider's view, bringing in new skills, adding to the team's diversity with new perspectives and the energy that a new recruit can bring to a team, are all strong reasons to go external.

When employers post a job externally it doesn't mean they haven't necessarily found what they want internally, but it might. Equally, when they haven't posted jobs externally, it doesn't mean they *have* found it internally. In fact, they may not realise they could benefit from what an external person has to bring, at least not yet. In short, there is no reason to wait for job postings.

The cheetah is driven by a simple urge: the need to eat and to provide for her cubs. The cheetah does not just sit and wait for wildebeest to line up in a procession while she takes her pick of the most appropriately-sized beast for dinner. If only life was so simple! Instead, she is required to put in both effort and experience to target the exact type of situation that will be most beneficial. I would argue that you can do the same thing in your job hunt if you choose.

Sharpen up your communication skills and give it a go. Remember that, as you approach a company, you are selling 'you', and as a sales person, you will get knock-backs. All sales people get knock-backs. You just have to learn to take them without getting knocked *down*. Go for it, you can do it!

Move upstream in the process for a catch

Having taken the time to work out what roles and environment work for you, try finding them before the job posting appears so as to be top of mind when opportunities are arising. This does not have to be an arduous task, but it does take commitment and focus. You might want to target a certain industry or companies in a certain location if this is something that is a key requirement from your list of needs.

I started by looking at the brands in my cupboards or at the services I use at home. This meant that I already endorse the products naturally as a customer, and I'd never have to pretend to like the products I make or sell. Having an idea of exactly where you might like to work is a concrete way of expressing your ideal environment, and in preparing the story of why you want that, you are communicating with commitment. With that much rationale, already you have enough to open a conversation with target employers.

Shortlist the companies you want to work for

Try flipping your perspective. Instead of looking for a job, interview companies to find one that fits your needs list. On the surface, this might sound quite arrogant, but done in the right way, it can show real initiative and creativity which can be appealing to future employers. It was this process that ultimately led me to join Amazon.

Amazon was a service I had used for many years before 2015. It was a lifeline to me when I worked in Poland. It was one of 10 companies I listed as being potential places that I thought could fit my work style and what I was looking to achieve. For each company on my list, I started by seeing which contacts I had there, starting with my own network. I reached out to these contacts and asked for a 15-minute conversation to understand about the culture of the company, nothing more. I was very surprised with the positive reactions that I got, which resulted in me having multiple conversations and learning a lot about ideal places and less ideal places for me. If I had a positive conversation, my goal was to find a new contact at the end of that phone call, to help me get more specific about the inner workings of those companies and what they may need. I clearly knew little of the culture behind the brands from the outside. The key in this process was to never ask for a job.

In the case of Amazon, after a number of conversations, I felt there was a good fit, and these conversations turned into something much more like formal interviews. Even at that point, though, there was no job specifically referenced. I was interviewed for my range of skills and abilities and my capacity to learn and adapt. The role I ended up taking was partially scoped to allow me to join at director level.

For the other companies on the list, I had positive meetings too. In fact, I had three potential job opportunities emerging at the same time. The process ironed out some of the most important things, i.e. the actual environment and the scope of the job. My network helped immensely during the process, and it helped to extend my network too.

Network, but not just when you need something

The approach I took in exploring companies was ultimately only possible because individuals willingly gave me their time. That was a resource I hadn't imagined could be so powerful, and yet it opened up a series of fruitful avenues. I give my time today to people who ask in the same way, be that colleagues, connections or head-hunters. It's another of life's two-way streets. Given how seldom we change jobs, remaining in contact and keeping your network alive is important; it's something to do continuously.

Learning about opportunities early means being connected or top of mind, whether that's recruiters, hiring managers themselves or friends who may be able to refer you. Research by LinkedIn shows that up to 70-85% of roles are filled by networking.[9] Employee referrals have increased dramatically over recent years too. Approximately a third of new recruits come via this channel.[10] Give your help if you want to receive help. If head-hunters hit a dead end every time they call, then guess what? They will stop calling. Armed with your knowledge of yourself and your ideal context, connect with head-hunters or recruiters so as to be on their books, and let people in your confidence circle know when you are searching and when you're not, but offer your help in return. Being specific about what you are looking for, and also where you may be able to connect them, will help them know what you do and don't want. In that way, you are respecting people's time.

Everyone can network

I get quite exasperated when people tell me they just aren't very good at networking or that networking is only for extroverts. That's simply not true. Many people hold the image of networking in their heads as having to make uncomfortable conversations with strangers over drinks. I can understand why that image might be daunting and unattractive, but that's not really the only type of networking. In fact, it's probably not one of the things I would even say is particularly valuable for networking. Try instead to see networking as a way of coming into contact with people with whom you share something in common for an exchange of views. These views may be social, semi-social or work-related. Try viewing networking as remaining in contact with people or bringing other people into contact with others where it's helpful. That is where networking manifests itself as a useful skill. If the thought of mingling with new people fills you with dread, try and find opportunities that will be less scary and where the content is perhaps something you love. Meeting people through charitable organisations or shared social activities or getting involved with committees or societies within your workplace are all networking activities! They're just not dressed up as networking, so might have flown under your radar.

Whether we recognise it or not, we are all far more connected by networks than we might first think. Perhaps you don't know somebody, but you will probably know somebody who knows somebody who does. Just being conscious of networking is already a start, and perhaps this is all you need to see yourself as a networker. It is, after all, a small world.

Engineer your digital match

Online job boards such as Monster, LinkedIn, Indeed, Totaljobs, company websites and the databases of recruiting companies will always have positions. Your task is to be informed and considered without losing relevance. If you've ever spent time searching these job-posting sites, you won't be surprised to see quite how many different positions are posted at any one time.

Using what you've learnt about yourself, take time to narrow down the types of opportunities you are interested in and look to match keywords within the job description back to your CV or the accompanying information that you supply about yourself. With high volumes of roles and applications, you can expect algorithms to do the work of matching and filtering.

Don't get overly hung up on job titles. Try and look past these, and focus on matching your skills to those required in the description to ensure you don't miss opportunities. For an efficient search, ensure your CV or resume highlights what you've done and the skills you have. Communicate what you are looking for with as much specificity as you can when using the options these platforms provide. As online recruiting services progress in their sophistication, head-hunters increasingly have a wealth of data and search capabilities at their fingertips, so it makes sense to ensure you are easy to 'find'. Ensure that when people search by connections, experience or industry, you appear for the relevant opportunities.

Step 7: Manage your first impression

Once you have found an opportunity that excites you, one that matches your needs and desires, remember to pause. In a busy marketplace, speed is of the essence. However, deciding how you would like to present yourself is equally important. There is a lot to be said for the phrase: 'You only get one chance to make a first impression.' It is very easy to manage this in a face-to-face interview, but the first connection with a potential employer is usually over a telephone call or via a digital interaction.

The application letter, email or call should set the tone you desire. Show confidence, showcase your offer and start to tailor it to the employer. Demonstrate how what you bring can benefit them, and above all, seek to pique the interest of the employer (or recruiter) to know more. Differentiate yourself from the crowd, and be you!

Start as you mean to go on

Now equipped with self-awareness and self-belief, it's important to be yourself through this final stage of the process, and yet it is so easy to hide the real you now that more is at stake. Worrying what to wear to an interview is common. Here's an example of just how different a perception you can create with your clothing. When interviewing at the end of my MBA, I was speaking with a range of companies, from consumer brands to strategy houses to investment banks. I decided to wear something that I felt like myself in. It is a personal choice, but I find that, when I'm comfortable with how I look, I perform better. Trivial perhaps, but powerful and my choice.

On this particular day, I chose to wear a red suit which consisted of a red dress and a red jacket. For the graduating students at my business school, there was a tradition of returning to the common room on campus and meeting with other people interviewing for jobs to debrief together. I can distinctly remember one of the other participants saying to me: 'Wow, they should have given you a job just for turning up in that outfit!' It was not lost on me how that particular individual, in his dark navy suit with blue and white shirt, looked the same as many others in the room. I do think that this snarky comment reflected more on the individual who made it than on me. Ultimately, I was proved right in my choice, as the interviews that day did turn into a job offer.

Deciding how to balance fitting an organisation's expectations with being true to yourself, at this early stage of getting acquainted, is a fine art. I was always taught that you can never overdress for an occasion but that you can underdress, and hence I've erred on the side of smart rather than casual for initial meetings. Some companies have a stricter dress codes than others, but it's important that you feel comfortable, so why not ask beforehand?

If the dress requirements are so extremely different to your own preferences, then perhaps this is a work environment that's not going to be a match for you. But, equally, if you are to have any hope of thriving as yourself and working in a way that suits you with this new company, there should be no need to unnecessarily hide who you are and how you come across. What is so much more important than your attire is that you are able to communicate with your true passion and share the perspectives that you have and the person that you are, with or without a uniform.

Step 8: Learn throughout the interview process

Once you get a firm confirmation of an interview, congratulate yourself for getting that far. It is easy to see the first interview as the start of the process. However, in a very competitive world, it is no small feat to have made it that far and to have secured a shot at an opportunity. With so many candidates to choose from, being selected to meet people is a win. Be it a telephone call or face-to-face conversation, you can be confident that you have already impressed your future employer and now you are entering the home straight.

This is by no means a point at which to ease off. The race intensifies to the finish line, and this is the time to really focus and get into the 'zone'. Do use that confidence you have built to draw breath and to give you the perspective that you need to ensure that you treat the interview process as part of a two-way street.

Any prospective employer needs to grill you to see who you are and that you can do the job, but it's also a chance for both parties to see if a working relationship will be fruitful. In short, this is your chance to see if the employer and this new role can meet the needs you have outlined for yourself.

Listen for the problems and demonstrate how you can help

All employers have problems to solve, and this is the moment to convert your skill set and capabilities into added value and provide solutions to their challenges. If it helps, think of the interview process as an invitation to tender for a contract. Letting the employer know you understand their challenges, and have thought about how you could help, will be well received. If you can, try to weave that thinking into your examples and answers in the interview. Make the interview about the employer and how you will benefit them. Do your homework beforehand to build as much insight as possible into their business challenges, then use the interview to delve deeper with questions. You do have to sell yourself as we have already noted, so remember your unique selling points (USPs) and build them in!

Ask questions

Every well-organised interview should, in my opinion, allow for time to take questions from the interviewee. It's, of course, an almost impossible ask to expect a candidate to know everything about a new company, a new manager and a new role from just the job advertisement and the job description. However, I'm continually surprised to hear candidates come forward with very few questions when the time comes. Not only does this signal to an employer a lack of interest in the company, but it could show that you're not able to be selective or display the confidence that you are choosing to actively seek employment with them, as opposed to just being grateful to have anything. The latter may well be the case in some situations, but don't display it. If employers can choose from many candidates, then a highly motivated one will be a better choice, so be that candidate.

If you are making a move to further your career, looking for somewhere which is better suited to you, then you should be actively seeking information in the interview stage and demonstrating a thirst to learn too.

It's quite easy to read up about the company and find out about their culture, whether that be from news articles or through connections that you have. It's also reasonably easy to anticipate the requirements of a job once the specifics are laid out in a decent job description. What is not possible, without at least having a conversation, is to understand how the hiring manager operates and what that could mean for your working context, should you be successful in the interview process. Given the impact of managers on the success of individuals, this is a crucial part of the process in finding the right position. It is, arguably, far harder to ask insightful questions of the manager once you are in the position because then the subordinate-and-manager relationship is in place.

By asking the manager upfront, in the interview, about their style, the team and how they work with them, you make a point of valuing and recognising the importance of their role in shaping your success. Think back to the criteria in the needs list in Chapter 3, and those for the manager, to ensure you ask the right questions. Far from making you look needy or aggressive, this display of confidence and self-awareness could be what separates you from the crowd. Ideally, the answers you get will describe the environment that you're looking for, but if the manager is not going to be working in a style that suits you, it would be far better that you learn that at the beginning. You can then choose to bow out or to continue with your eyes open and seek to fix or compensate for any differences in style later.

Interview for a career, not a job

Companies invest a huge amount of time in recruiting external candidates, and it is reasonable to expect, therefore, that they wish you to be successful and satisfied, not only in the job which you are interviewing for but in successive roles. They want you to build a career with that company. To that end, it's advisable to ask about development opportunities and future progress or promotion prospects, in order for you to understand how those processes work. Remember that many people leave their employers because of the lack of opportunities or the lack of learning and growth. In fact, millennials reportedly value opportunities to progress and the chance to be mentored almost as highly as compensation and benefits, and five times more than flexible working.[11] So, be specific, if possible, about what you would hope for, to ensure that the organisation can deliver on your future expectations and not just the job. At the end of the day, if you find a work environment that you thrive in, it would only be natural that you would look for additional opportunities over time.

Step 9: Don't take rejections personally

Given the statistics around job hunting and the funnelling of potential candidates down to the final candidate, it means that rejections are a normal part of the process. It is easy to forget this when you're on the receiving end of a 'no'. Remember that you have been pitching your skills to potential customers, and not all tenders result in a sale. Some of the best sales people I know are brilliant at accepting a 'no'. Expect there to be a certain proportion of 'nos' before a 'yes' is found. No product has a 100% conversion rate.

Should you reach a dead end in an interview process, look to learn from it so that you don't leave that particular process without anything. Ask for feedback to understand where the mismatch in capabilities and expectations lies, or to understand what other candidates potentially had that you didn't. Having hired a number of people in my time, I know that sometimes requirements which may have nothing to do with you personally are reasons for rejection. The desire to have resources on board under a tight timeframe, or on a limited budget, is not uncommon. This may mean that considerations that are not necessarily an indication of your capabilities may indeed be drivers of final decisions.

I was lucky, across the career moves I made in the early years, to not have too many failed attempts, at least not once I got an interview. I did get more rejections to the postal applications I made, where my CV failed to make it onto the shortlist – the engineer applying for commercial roles dilemma again! – that served to help me sharpen my materials and my rationale.

The first time I applied for a job, interviewed, and then didn't get it, was for a job post-MBA. I had applied to too many in the on-campus recruitment, and it is clear now that some of them were never really 'for me' and that I could have seen that with more research upfront. The next 'failure' (or learning opportunity) was an internal move at Amazon. Strangely, I was under time pressure to make a move due to certain organisational changes which led me to consider roles that might not have been top of my list. Not everything on the top of my list was available at the moment, but that's life! I lost out to an internal candidate for whom I have enormous respect and who fully deserved the job. In asking for feedback about my own interviews and where the shortcomings were, I was very surprised to learn that pretty much the only objection was that one individual on the interview panel had felt that I didn't seem confident.

Of all the things that I could think of, confidence is not something which I lack, and that made me step back and wonder why I had left that impression. The recruiting manager will never be able to answer that fully, as given feedback is anonymous. What I did learn in looking at that whole process was that, even when I think I'm in control of the enthusiasm that I'm bringing to an interview process, I don't fully hide my true motivations. While I did want that job, I didn't want it badly enough. Somehow that must have come through in my mannerisms or in the confidence with which I chose and then brought to life my examples.

This was a valuable learning experience for me, so it certainly wasn't a wasted exercise. Keeping that positive perspective is important, however you explain it to yourself. You will be successful at some point and secure an offer.

Step 10: Check your needs before you accept

If your primary reason for making an external move is to improve your career prospects and meet needs that were missing for you in your current or previous roles, then you may have a number of options in play if you have spread your net wide. Understanding how to choose between the options is a challenge, so reflect back to find the best fit. If you've gone through the process of documenting all the elements of self-awareness, your goals and your descriptions of needs, then it should be very easy to compare job offers and to bring into view all the different elements that each job will contain.

I used a similar process when I reached out to Nike after business school. Of the multiple offers I landed, this was the one opportunity I had created myself, and it felt like me. Having gone to business school to move back to industry and buy flexibility for the future, this made sense. My gut feel told me to follow my passion and move to a new country again, rather than accept one of the other offers that were more 'blue suit'. Although those offers would have paid my study fees, the restriction of a further two years of not being myself was too costly, and so I extended my financial loan, self-funded my study and instead followed my gut. I was not disappointed.

Not everything will be top of mind as you review a job contract, so step back. Doing this in a neutral way will help you make a decision in the event your internal compass isn't telling you which one is better for you. Even when you have an undeniable calling for one over another, it's a good check to revisit that list of needs to ensure you have what is required to be fulfilled. Recognise the starting point of a new journey so you are able to reflect back on it later in case, at some point in the future, your needs start to be unmet.

Is the wrong job better than no job?

When presented with only one offer, you may not think of it as a decision. I would still recommend reflecting on your needs criteria to ensure you go into the next role with your eyes open on the shortcomings of the role versus your minimum requirements. In that way, you clearly recognise what is missing and accept it as a choice that you yourself make before embarking on the new role. This makes it easier to accept and to work with those shortcomings, rather than let them boil up and frustrate you in the new role. Remember the element of choice you have in experiencing frustrations and stress.

Personally, I do think having no job is sometimes better than having the wrong job. This is if, of course, your financial situation can withstand it. The wrong context can be a cause of lasting damage, disappointment or certainly short-term stress, depending on the key needs that are not going to be met for you.

At least twice in my career I have found myself part of a restructure; you may be surprised how common these are. In one situation, while at Amazon, my role became redundant. I would like to say that Amazon is not only a massive, multidimensional company, but it's also extremely flexible. Amazon encourages employees to move around, to learn different angles of the business, to be curious and to build different career paths. This can work well, but less well under time restrictions.

I found myself without a role and evaluating alternatives which were proposed to me rather than those that I sought out. It was great that Amazon didn't want to lose me as a valuable employee, but it didn't mean that every role I was asked to consider would be right for me or interest me, nor that the one I was targeting would be available at the time my move happened.

I have a strong vision of my career path, having built up self-awareness over many years. I know which skills I like using and what I'm passionate about. I have learnt the types of teams, and in particular managers, that work well for me and, of course, the topic of the job itself is important. It was therefore quite easy for me to see which jobs were not a good fit for me. I have to say that my then manager and HR colleagues reacted with some level of surprise that I turned down not just one, but two different roles in that situation. I was sailing close to the wind, passing up opportunities in order to hold out for something more suitable though running out of time to secure a new role. I did eventually land a role, so that chapter comes to a happy end. It was a risk, but one I was comfortable with, despite how bizarre others found it. Let me ask you this: if you wanted to have dessert after dinner in a restaurant, but of the many choices on the menu nothing appealed to you, and indeed some dishes contained ingredients that could make you unwell, would you take one anyway or pass on dessert? With enough self-awareness, you can spot the jobs and contexts 'on the menu' that you should sometimes pass on too. The day I simply accept that I am lucky to have a job, and that the choice shouldn't matter, will be the day I lose confidence in myself, and I hope that day never arrives.

Run to, not from

If, unlike that example, you are evaluating external moves while still in your current position, moving towards the wrong job for you could be worse than taking your time and spending a little longer in your current role. If you are moving to fix a context challenge, it is possible to repeat the situation you are looking to leave behind unless you look at it dispassionately as you decide. Ask yourself, is the new job appealing, and is it right for you? Be honest. Also ask yourself how long you think it might be until you find yourself back in the position you are in right now, missing something and seeking a move? If your answer to the last question is a reasonably short amount of time, then perhaps this is not the right move for you and waiting would be more productive in the long run.

Don't lose it in the contractual negotiations

Until you have signed your contract, everything is still in play. Remember back to how you scoped your ideal role and your minimum criteria, including the things which help you thrive. The majority of things that matter go beyond the standard contractual details. As you approach a new job offer, instead of focusing your energy in only negotiating compensation and other standard terms and conditions, make sure you check back in with the full suite of needs that you have.

Have you checked what the learning opportunities are, the flexible working arrangements, relocation or commuting compensations or even the diversity and inclusion policies? There are many things to consider when signing up to the entire offer, and now is the time to review them. The moment after you are offered the job and before you sign is the largest point of leverage you are going to have. Given how much effort and cost this potential employer has already invested to get this far in the process, there is likely to be more flexibility in order to get the deal over the line. I'm not suggesting that you go into deep negotiations over unrealistic things, but if you do have any undiscussed needs at that point, it makes sense to see if they can be accommodated.

I have met individuals who felt they missed out on a benefit like flexible working hours, remote working or training resources, which they never mentioned nor requested. Their starting assumption was it would not be allowed and so they didn't check. Believe in yourself and stand firm, but give good reasons why you would like to ask for alternative things. If they're necessary and important, then look to have them baked into a contract at the beginning.

Hopefully now you have found a job that fits you, and it is

awesome to get to this point. Once you reach this stage, celebrate not only the fact that you found your job, but that you did it from a drive to be yourself. Share not just the success, but how you did it and what you did differently. Looking back and seeing what you achieved, before diving headlong into the new challenge, will serve you well. You will be stronger the next time you need to make a change. Go ahead and savour the moment. Commit it to memory and you will build your confidence for the future.

6

The Career Pivot

THE MOST common form of job hunt is one that searches for something similar to your current job. This often happens when individuals realise they are not having all their needs met and they jump to fix specific elements. However, you might be missing a trick if you only look for the same roles. Having arrived at this crossroads, why not look at the crazy options as well as the well-trodden path, or at least consider them to confirm the direction you are taking? Embarking on a completely new career, whether that be a totally new industry or starting a business of your own or even inheriting one, could be your thing.

Working for yourself

Looking at the explosion in start-ups and entrepreneurs, there's inspiration in abundance if you have an idea and you want to make it happen. Equally, the world of interim workers or portfolio workers who want to do the same work but on completely different terms, choosing flexibility in their work patterns, over the security of a permanent contract, show that the self-employed world is booming. Technology makes things possible today that were unimaginable only a few years ago. If you have an idea, a laptop and an internet connection, then you can pretty much start anything.

Given that the journey is very likely to be bumpier than being in constant employment, both in terms of the challenges and in financial continuity, it won't be for everyone, and it carries more risk. But, if you are OK with that, or if you in fact thrive on it, then go for it. If you are considering this, then I wish you the best of luck and an exciting journey!

I worked for myself very briefly. I had made what we shall call a suboptimal decision in my career, one which saw it derail momentarily, and so I began working for myself as a way of continuing in employment. It gave me space to understand what had happened and what I wanted next while also keeping busy. It was also a way of holding onto my employment status while being based in a country where I wasn't a national. Neither of those are solid reasons to go into the world of working for yourself. To be honest, it just sort of happened. I motored along, got some interim or consulting assignments which were quite varied, met some interesting people and paid the bills. My final assignment as a self-employed individual, one which came to me via a networking exchange, was for McCormick, a company where I later went on to have seven very fruitful years as a direct employee. I wasn't looking to work for myself, I wasn't driven to work for myself and I wasn't a great fan of the amount of administration that came with it, but I did at least learn that it wasn't for me at that time.

I didn't have a fantastic product idea that justified me starting a company at that time, something that might have made more sense as a business, so I simply did similar, interim work, but from my own company. Working for myself doesn't feature high enough on my goal list, nor did it meet needs I couldn't meet in the traditional employment context. It was a brief experience where I learned about myself. It hasn't hurt my career and hence I didn't have a great deal to lose by trying it. So, if you are unsure as to whether it will be for you, perhaps give it a go. If you can identify a need in your work environment or context that *would* be met in that way, then perhaps it could be right for you.

Portfolio work

It is not uncommon to do a number of jobs or self-employed endeavours alongside each other to satisfy your multiple needs. When I look at the jobs at McCormick and Amazon that were most fulfilling, they consisted of a busy 'day job', plus one or even two other roles. This was sometimes a project, sometimes an executive sponsorship for a cross-business drive like diversity or even my role as UK spokesperson for Amazon. Each one added something that was not present in the 'day job'. This gave me the variety that I required. I also added external, non-executive roles and volunteering, both of which gave me additional stretch and a chance to give back too. With all these possibilities, albeit some were within the same company in my example, it is very easy to see how it becomes possible to build a career without a full-time 'day job', should you so wish.

As long as your needs are met, there is no reason why a job in the traditional sense should be the answer for you. So, explore your own unique set of needs and the potential ways to gain fulfilment and meet the financial or other requirements that you have. There is no limit to creativity; perhaps the portfolio option is another way of learning about yourself as you go.

Switching out or off for a while

There is no rule that says employment needs to be continuous throughout your life for you to be fulfilled. I know plenty of individuals who have had a very fruitful and valuable time away from paid employment. If you can afford it, and your self-awareness and understanding of what situations fulfil you draw you in a particular direction, then arriving at the conclusion that you would like to focus on something else for a while is as valuable as knowing what you'd like to target for your next job.

Today's job market is so full of change that experiences from many angles will always be valued. Just as we touched on in the 'Sell the gap in your employment' section earlier, time doing something different to your career does not have to be a dead end in terms of prospects. Not only is it about how you sell that when you return to the workforce, but it's also about understanding why you desired that in the first place. This knowledge is a huge piece of maintaining your own personal drive or ambition in life.

When changes in my context happened, I began to miss some key needs and, rather than stay in a situation that wasn't working for me, I paused full-time employment to write this book. I haven't stopped loving what I do as a leader, but I have created an opportunity to scale some of that coaching via my book, while taking time to do some reflection myself. It wasn't planned exactly as it worked out, as will be true for many 'time outs', but knowing that I am in control of my story, as you will be too, it didn't matter. Regardless of how you spend your time out of the 'rat race', whether by accident or by design, it's important to remember that it is a valid piece of your journey. It is another experience which will add to your diversity as an individual. Embrace the chance to do something different and notice what you learn about yourself. It could provide huge insight and an avenue to somewhere completely different; a new beginning for you. Equally, it could confirm, quite harshly, that it's a dead end and that you are more comfortable in the surroundings of an employment contract. Nothing ventured, nothing gained; so the best advice is to enjoy it.

Once you are ready to enter back into the world of employment, if indeed this is what you want, whether a new job or the launch of a new venture, then a quick refresh of your product map and needs list will help you hit the ground running, as will your likely recharged battery.

7

The Internal Move

MUCH OF what we have already covered about the job hunt process will also be applicable to internal moves, particularly in very large organisations where internal candidates are encouraged to move, even to areas within the organisation which may be quite far apart. In a company of sufficient size, this can almost feel like an external move. If you have found a company that ticks the boxes for you on many fronts and it is somewhere you can imagine staying for a long period, then setting up for an internal move, even at some future point, is a good idea. Very few people will remain fulfilled working in the exact same role and team forever, nor will companies likely encourage this. Actively managing your internal career is therefore the best course of action to stay engaged and fulfilled. Here are some steps to help you consider how.

Tip 1: Learn the process

One thing is certain: all organisations have their own process for internal moves; but what is also certain is that these steps will not be followed, strictly, 100% of the time. Find out from your manager, HR team, colleagues and those who you have seen made moves, how they tend to happen in your organisation. Understanding the requirements to be considered for a move, and the typical moments they happen, will ensure you don't miss the boat. Performance ratings, tenure, readiness and future potential can all count. Check whether all jobs are posted internally and what level of manager involvement or support you need. Some organisations are less formal about this than others. However, as the focus on equitable treatment of employees is elevated, expect this to get more structured, even in the less formal environments.

I have worked for companies whose internal progression processes are at both ends of the scale in terms of formality. Most companies will have HR processes to measure performance and reward and grow talent, ensuring that potential leaders and top achievers are nurtured and fuelled with opportunities. These processes also ensure that those not keeping up with the pack are developed or encouraged to look elsewhere.

During my time in the larger consumer goods companies, the processes were quite structured and talent was reviewed on an HR grid. Opportunities were lined up for individuals with roles or potential moves effectively sketched out, at least hypothetically. Career paths that demonstrated typical routes from A to B over many years were also not uncommon. At Amazon, although talent is also reviewed structurally, the career planning was far more fluid. The difference, in my experience, comes with how moves happened in practice. I made as many moves in McCormick as I did at Amazon, so let's compare them.

On the one hand, at McCormick, my name found its way

onto a shortlist because of my performance or my career aspirations, and in some cases, my geographic mobility or language
capability. I also had a sponsor, and so opportunities came to
me. I am most grateful for the chances I was given by McCormick
to run the Dutch business, and I was extremely happy to be
approached to run the Polish acquisition too. I loved the element of choice I had when I was approached to move into the
northern Europe position. All these positions were moves that
were suggested to me, opportunistically.

At Amazon, on the other hand, the moves which I made were
all ones that I had to apply for. Although Amazon has the same
HR processes, or similar ones, every job is essentially considered as
an open vacancy for almost anybody across the business to apply
for, with certain prerequisites. This works well as it ensures great
mobility across the business and cross-fertilisation of ideas. What
this does mean, however, is that in order to benefit from moves as
they became 'available', I had to understand the process in order
to have my name considered. Having hired many individuals
within Amazon myself, I knew you didn't just leave it to the
internal noticeboard to scoop a shortlist of candidates. I reached
out to people that I'd heard of to see if they would be interested.
However, the process is wide open.

The point here is to get to understand the DNA of the organisation that you're working with, and find out about the reality
beyond the HR processes. How do people actually land the moves
which they make, and how can you?

Tip 2: Be active, plan and let your needs be known

Don't expect the work of navigating your career internally to be
done for you. It is your responsibility. Keeping your eyes and ears
open and managing your internal move is a must. If you have

a vision for where you want to be, say in five years' time, that's great. If not, then start thinking about what you would like to do or to have achieved.

Make a plan and discuss it with your current manager. Some companies have their own preferred systems or forms, and it helps to work within that. Some are reviewed at talent meetings and others are tagged to match future opportunities if they are held digitally. Make sure you know how any such plans will be used and by whom or whether they are for self-reflection only. There is nothing wrong with being ambitious, but make sure you keep it realistic and recognise what it takes to make the next steps successfully.

Plan concrete steps to acquire the skills and experience you will need and get commitment from your manager to support you. As with all plans, put some timeframes against it or it is all too easy to coast. Make sure the business is aware of your preferences around mobility and capabilities in terms of languages, as these can open up a different set of opportunities that otherwise wouldn't be available to you in your current location. Languages and mobility are sometimes a real differentiator, certainly one I have benefitted from having. If you don't yet have a certain language capability, even sharing your appetite to learn one can help.

Just like the process for the external hunt, your CV and story are crucial and still something that you can maintain for internal moves. In larger organisations, don't expect everyone to know instantly who you are or what you are looking for. Whether it is exploratory conversations with new parts of the business or internal interview processes, ensure you line up your materials to do yourself justice!

Tip 3: Build your results; build your reputation

Regardless of how you move, whether between roles, teams, business units or geographies, it all comes at a price to an employer, both in terms of the learning curve and the practical costs. So, understand that this is an investment in you. It is reasonable to expect that, to gain such an opportunity, you should be performing well in your current role, so ensure you are delivering against your targets. Delivering results is not just a strong start to being able to move, but also a feature that will count in your favour against the competition. Ensure, therefore, that your achievements do not go unnoticed.

There's nothing wrong with a little shameless self-promotion, in my book. Men are often better than women at this, so don't be shy ladies! Don't expect other people to blow your trumpet if you're not willing to blow it yourself from time to time. Striking the right tone is the challenge. Think of the value of sharing best practice or scaling ideas that work instead of just highlighting that you have achieved great things. Perhaps share that news with a view to how others could do the same or learn from what you did to give some insight back. Team, department or town hall meetings, email updates or newsletters can all be neutral ways of sharing success stories, and you might find editors are all too willing to include your content if you volunteer.

If you are a manager yourself, recruiting, developing and promoting your own people is a great track record to have, so ensure you treat others as you would like to be treated and invest in your team. Celebrating success with awards (employee of the month, star of the week, etc.) is a good way to give people visibility, so nominate others to acknowledge their work if you also want recognition. Having a name for getting stuff done and attracting and developing talent will make you a highly sought-after person. Whatever it is you want to be known for, take steps to be that, to show that and to share it.

Tip 4: Get involved in the organisation

Companies invest in employees who do more than just a good job. I'm not suggesting that the only way to get ahead is to do more than just the day job, but ask yourself whether you are committed to this organisation beyond your current role? Getting involved in things beyond your current responsibilities shows that you care about the success of the company. It is never too soon to start giving. The extra effort could be mentoring people from other teams or it could be volunteering to sit on committees or get involved in organising some of the social events. It's about being part of the culture which you already enjoy in order to build a career and not just a job at the company.

Don't draw the line at supporting things internally as there is a great deal you can do to represent the company, externally, as an ambassador. Getting involved in these extra activities is not something to do simply because you want to make an internal move, but because it also gives you a different development angle and, importantly, it can be hugely rewarding.

Over my career, I have represented the company through activities as diverse as running races for charity, attending charity events, speaking at external events, taking part in industry forums and hosting events on behalf of the company. I've also taken part in external recruiting and sat on panels of experts judging competitions. I even found myself on BBC News to help increase the number of women in innovation, and I took part in the TV show, *Buy It Now*, with Rylan Clark, investing in budding entrepreneurs while representing Amazon Launchpad. Yes, the list really is eclectic.

It's about finding time and being willing to invest it in areas where you have something to offer, as part of being proud to work for the company. These things are not compulsory, of course; I see them as exciting extras which were appreciated and which I enjoyed doing. They might even have counted as networking!

Tip 5: Add to the day job

If you are thinking of an internal move because you are missing something in your current role, then you could take steps to fill that need gap while you're already in your current job. The types of needs that involve growth, development, stimulation or challenge often have a number of solutions, some far easier to solve than the upheaval of moving departments or business units. In the companies that I have worked for the longest, and coincidentally had the most internal moves, I always had projects or responsibilities in addition to the day job. Far from being an added burden, these extra roles gave me something that wasn't possible to get in my main job, either because of its scope or because of the moment in time.

At McCormick, I was lucky to be part of the multiple management board (MMB), which is an internal programme that involved working on projects together with peers around the globe. This opportunity not only gives you a diversion from the day job but, importantly, it connects you with individuals around the organisation, strengthening ties with colleagues in a company where you intend to build a future. Such projects are great two-way streets: the organisation benefits from you applying your skills in a different dimension; and, of course, it brings together diversity of thought to provide inspiration and sources of innovation while working on current business problems.

The same is true for Amazon, where I had a sponsor role and

kicked off the collaboration process between Amazon Retail and Amazon Advertising in Europe (both very separate companies). This was something I did alongside my director responsibilities, and it was a little like being an external consultant as well as an employee. In this case it also paved the way to me working much more closely with advertising years later.

Totally unconnected from my day job at Amazon, I also helped shape the drive for diversity and inclusion in the UK as the executive sponsor for diversity. Both those opportunities let me create something new on a blank page; to build something that didn't exist. It let me create and explore in a way that was different to the slightly more prescriptive, day-to-day management and meticulous execution I was used to within the retail business. Moreover, from the diversity role sprang a whole new responsibility for me in the UK as an official spokesperson for the business. This was something that I would not have dreamt of doing as a full-time job but which I was extremely proud to take on and which I thoroughly enjoyed.

Through these extra roles, the business gets to know you as an individual, your equity increases as your visibility increases and you can push yourself to demonstrate different dimensions that would otherwise go unseen in the scope of the day job. What all of those extra roles did for me was to keep me at my maximum engagement to offset the decreasing challenge as I mastered the day job. Inadvertently, this made me more patient for an internal opportunity to emerge that could address my needs.

So, look around you and see which skills or needs you would like to address and how you could start to do that with something incremental in your current role rather than only looking for a career move. Who knows, maybe the additional task is something you excel at so much so that it becomes your next role!

Tip 6: Not all jobs exist, yet

Business is constantly changing, and although it may not be apparent, organisational structures are continually changing too. Whether it's efficiency, profitability, centralisation, decentralisation, transformational change or new growth, the drivers for organisational change are endless. Roles are created, removed, combined or rescoped almost continually, if you look over a long time period. Therefore, targeting a particular role is not always going to be fruitful.

This is why it's so important to understand your toolkit and your ambitions and to be flexible as companies evolve. When I worked at Nike, the department I started in was strategic planning. In fact, I was the first employee in it. The idea was that this department, or team as it later became, was itself created as a springboard into the rest of the business. It was a good entry point as it gave you a bird's eye view, the opportunity to work on a mix of business topics and report to senior directors with board visibility.

That was a two-way street in terms of visibility, with each project being sponsored by one of the board. I was most fortunate to find that not only could I see the business opportunities, but I was even able to scope a strategic opportunity, and then got the chance to go and build it, moving over to the commercial sales teams to do so. This was a great example of understanding the process and literally creating my own next step. I have certainly learnt never to suggest anything I am not willing to go and do myself. You never know when someone might actually hand you the opportunity, resources and freedom to make it happen.

Tip 7: Be selective; it's OK to say 'no'

When you're building a reputation for yourself, it's only natural that you may be approached with opportunities. (Congratulations, you are in the opportunity box from the grid in Chapter 5!) It is indeed a real compliment to be sought out by somebody. However, ensure to detach yourself from that moment to question neutrally and dispassionately whether the option is something for you. There is little benefit in accepting something that you are not convinced is right. So, always show appreciation when people reach out to you with opportunities, and by all means evaluate them thoroughly, but stand firm to politely reject things which you don't feel are true to what you are searching for at that moment. I often wonder how things may have evolved if I had turned down the move at McCormick that relocated me from Poland back to the head office in the UK. With that experience under my belt, I reflect more and I have much less of a problem saying 'no'.

Amazon is rich with opportunities, and I had to turn some down when moving on beyond my initial role as director of toys for Germany. I even interviewed for one role which, although it was the right level, was too far from where my true passion lay in terms of focus. I only felt this after having completed the interview process, learning about the role beyond the title as I progressed. I pondered, and then dug deep and politely turned it down, explaining to the hiring manager why. It felt very painful to do so, as if I was letting the side down. However, it meant I was patient and available, not long afterwards, to get the role I really wanted. It was a position which didn't yet exist – a new European role, leading the beer, wines and spirit business.

Again, drawing on your self-awareness, finding the right words to have that conversation, to politely appreciate and yet turn down an opportunity, is a valuable skill. There is no shame in knowing what you are looking for.

Tip 8: Build stepping stones to learn and grow

Having decided to commit to an extended period of time at your current company, you can view your moves as steps towards a certain goal rather than seeing each step as a discrete goal itself. In taking this view, you gain a great deal of flexibility to chart a path towards a certain future job, building yourself different routes which you could take. Some companies may do this for you, albeit with a generic career path in mind.

Learning and personal growth comes from a place of discomfort, not a familiar groove. To develop it, take the opportunities of adjacent moves now and then. Not all moves need to be straight up with increasing seniority. In fact, some steps along your path may need you to do at least a couple of different roles *before* progressing.

Remember the value of diversity as a source of innovation. You will gain new perspectives when trialling new things, new teams and new disciplines. It is powerful to see an organisation through the eyes of different teams and also to see how a customer is serviced through different parts of a business. The experience you gain while building these stepping stones can be invaluable, so consider what it is you would like to see from a new vantage point to support you in your end goal.

For those millennials looking for justification that a quick 'climb of the ladder' is the only route to success, slow down. Moving roles does not always mean upwards and onwards. I am advocating variation. This is not to say that a rapid rise is not possible. Rather, you need to put in the legwork to gain the right depth of experience and be open to gaining that experience in multiple roles or companies.

Tip 9: Get your supporters on board

Ownership for your career lies ultimately with you, but good managers, mentors and sponsors can play a big part in helping you move at the right moment. Draw on your self-awareness, and be honest with yourself about where you need support or guidance. There are a range of supporters who can help you find and secure good internal moves, as well as developing yourself for a longer career in the company.

Manager

Getting your manager involved is not only advisable but can, in some organisations, be a way of getting ahead of the game. Your manager may be privy to opportunities long before positions become public knowledge, whether it's opportunities, emerging restructures, new investments or resignations. Some of the best managers I've worked with are great at building career plans for their teams and securing them opportunities.

With your manager engaged in your plan, they can provide valuable feedback on skills, experience or the exposure needed for you to open up opportunities. Your manager also has different visibility upwards and across the organisation, so try to make the most of that. They can put your name in the hat at key moments of consideration as they arise, sometimes long before you may hear of them.

Ensure that you both share the same view of your direction of travel, and importantly, your readiness to take on something additional. In the event you disagree with your manager on your readiness, be sure to get a concrete commitment as to what is needed to close the gap.

Mentor

A mentor's independent advice or use as a sounding board can be invaluable as you plot a career path within a company. If you have chosen your mentor as somebody who can open doors and can connect you, not only can they help shape you to get ready for a move, but they may be the source of the opportunity itself. In the event of stiff competition for a new role, a mentor may be able to provide an additional voice of support, sometimes of value where you don't have the support of your manager.

While at Amazon, I had two mentors during my first few years, both of whom were able to help me find additional opportunities and also challenge me to answer whether they were the right ones for me. The latter was extremely valuable, such was the difference in ways of working at Amazon versus my prior experience. It helped me avoid making any assumptions about how things could turn out, and it expanded my own horizons as to quite how flexible the company could be and how widely, throughout the organisation, I could look for moves.

Sponsor

A sponsor is slightly different to the role of manager or mentor. A sponsor is normally associated with securing moves upwards in an organisation where otherwise you might struggle without some senior assistance. Sponsors take a more active role in supporting you, and crucially, they are there to advocate for you in your absence and can guide you through a company. Sponsors are often assigned to individuals that have been identified as potential high growth or top talent, to ensure they are able to navigate the organisation rather than leave for other opportunities.

You can, however, identify and ask someone to sponsor you. If a sponsor has an interest in your progression, it is a relationship that needs to be developed and valuable for them. Be patient and work to identify and secure one.

During my time in McCormick, I was grateful to have a mentor who turned into my manager for one role. They then subsequently put me in contact with a board sponsor who wanted to help develop individuals to senior level. With this visibility, I was very lucky to have my name put in the hat for an opportunity even while I was on maternity leave, so I had a great role to come back to. Having stakeholders in the business support you in this way is a huge luxury. Be mindful of their time, and give back where you can to respect the dynamic of the relationship.

Tip 10: Build talent behind you

As you prepare and navigate your own moves, use your learnings to develop your team's talent as you go. Remember that an organisation's assets are its employees, so this should be a win-win on your path to create the next move. Preparing a successor, or a few successors, can ensure that you move on smoothly and you don't leave chaos in your wake. Using the opportunity to bring people along with you is an excellent way of leaving positively. Gaining a reputation for developing people will stand you in good stead, both in securing a role and attracting talent into your team. It is never too soon to give back.

Share, connect, repeat

It is easy to cut all ties and head off to the new challenge, department or business, but remember that you are now an example of how to do it. Given that internal processes for changing departments or getting promoted are some of the biggest 'unwritten rules' inside organisations, it will help others to see examples of success. When you have gone through this, remember to give back and share what you've learnt as and when it is required. From participating in internal panels at development courses to supporting the induction programmes or indeed the recruitment efforts of the organisation, share your experience with pride.

As an example of someone who has moved internally, you can expect to be contacted for tips and advice. If this happens to you, my advice would be to share what you know. Never forget how it feels to be 'new' to a company or 'in the dark' about how things work. That way, you stay enthusiastic to enlighten and indeed motivate those who contact you.

> **Reflection – Create learning opportunities**
> If you have made an internal move, did it happen in the way the process was laid out? If not, how can you help others learn from this?

8

The Promotion

ONE INTERNAL move that changes your environmental context far more than some can be the promotion. Securing a promotion will likely follow the same steps as an internal move, albeit there may be specific criteria to meet in terms of training, experience, feedback and achievements. Once you get it, however, it will require you to reflect and adapt and, in this case, to be successful. Adapting is not optional.

Promotions look different in different organisations. Sometimes a promotion is a means to secure a role at the next level up, but sometimes it's about achieving a certain level of capability in the same role, from which you can then find alternate roles or become more of an expert in the same role.

The lay of the land changes in many ways once you move up, so in order to continue performing and being fulfilled, you need to acknowledge the challenge and adapt. There are a couple of scenarios where the self-reflection of mirror one and the reinforcement of mirror two will be critical to continued success. Revisiting your self-awareness will help you to recognise where your new learning lies and ensure you are tuned in to the new relationships that you will build with the team. Equally, setting out to do the new role with confidence and as yourself is a chance not to be missed.

The challenges faced after promotion differ depending on whether you move into a new team or gain a new position in the same team, and crucially, what this means for the people you may go on to manage.

First-time manager

Being promoted into your first role as a manager is a distinct moment of change. As you move away from being in charge of your own time, your own achievements and your own motivations, you now need to work through others. The behaviours that got you this far as an individual contributor are no longer the ones that will see you succeed as a manager. Being capable of self-awareness will help you to understand how and where you need to adapt and keep you attuned to how well you are able to meet the team's needs.

Gaining the respect and trust of your team is key, so being comfortable with who you are, and self-assured, will help you set strong foundations. Reflect on how you work: what type of manager are you going to be? Instructing people to do something versus motivating them are two different things. The latter involves a great deal more trust and influence, something which comes from a place of self-belief and in understanding how to listen to and read people.

Planning time for the anticipated, as well as the unexpected, needs of others as well as building relationships that open the avenues of feedback that you and the team need, are just two of the big changes you'll need to embrace. Having the self-belief to let go of your own performance and put it in the hands of others takes some getting used to as well.

Finding the balance of helping people to see the solution, as opposed to telling them what it is, does not come instantly to everyone, so be patient with yourself. Many new managers don't make this transition successfully, and it often comes down to a lack of their self-awareness or ability to seek feedback and adapt.

Manager of peers

Promotion to a position that requires you to manage colleagues that were previously your peers, whether you were already a manager or not, is another hurdle that is best attacked with self-awareness. Being aware of how you are perceived, and of your own feelings as you interact in a new way with your new team, will help you build trust. Ensuring you remain confident, but not overly so, can unite the team, but you also need to make sure you are sensitive in dealing with colleagues who may have felt the role was theirs and are dealing with disappointment.

When I moved into one role as president of the board in Poland, not everyone accepted my presence in that role initially. This was made apparent by small cues and not-so-subtle comments. In this environment, previously, the president of the board had always placed their diary at the top of the table. At the beginning of every meeting, I didn't place my diary at the head of the table and, for a number of weeks, I simply took a place on the right, closer to the front of the room. Colleagues brought to my attention the importance of that action in their culture. I hadn't considered where I sat around the table to be that important. Never having been part of such a visibly hierarchical environment, I was indifferent to where most people sat. What I did notice, however, was that despite the control and direction of the board being in my hands, and of course shared with my team, the individual sitting in the seat at the head of the table often behaved as if they were in control. It was not until I took that specific seat, and placed my belongings at the head of the table for each meeting, that behaviours gradually changed.

What is important in this example is that gaining acceptance as the new leader meant being aware of how others were signalling or behaving and not only doing what I felt was necessary or comfortable for me. It emerged later that this move signalled so much more to other people in the room, some of whom relied on its significance to adjust their own approach. I came to appreciate that fact with feedback from another colleague, who shared that with me in my one-on-one meetings. Had I been stubborn, less open-minded to changing things and unwilling to look beyond meeting my own needs, we may well have had a head-on collision.

So, as you make that transition to managing peers, use your confidence and self-belief alongside your ability to reflect. Try to see more than the visible emotions to ensure that you strike a new contractual relationship with peers: one that allows individuals to fail gracefully, if necessary, but which does not compromise the leadership required of you.

Whatever type of promotion you secure, whether it's increased responsibility, a subject matter expert or management, to succeed in making the transition, it helps to be humble, to take time to adjust and to remember that you are being thrown into the deep end again. The steepest part of the learning curve is at the start of a new challenge, and the longer you can stay in that area of discomfort, the bigger your total learning will be. As you grow in your role as manager, you can use your new vantage point to develop your team's self-awareness and encourage them to be themselves too!

9

The 'Bad' Manager

HAVING ADDRESSED some of the big career moves in the previous chapters, there is one key piece of the career fulfilment 'puzzle' missing. This context change can be the start of a move or simply a major adaptation, such is the effect on your job and even your life. When your needs go unmet, a common reaction is to focus on the job as the issue and jump into action to find a new one. Yet it would be remiss not to call out the elephant in the room, one that accompanies many a career change for people: that of the 'bad' manager, or in some cases, simply the 'bad for you' manager.

There are many types of manager, some better than others, and there are many styles of management, some better suited to different situations than others. However, there is no getting away from the fact that managers have a huge impact on the work world around you, and this can be a good or a bad thing. Managers have a responsibility, not only for the work that needs doing but for the engagement and development of their team members and for shaping the team environment. Good managers deliver results, and in my view, they remove hurdles so that their employees can be their best. Managers can be instrumental in helping, coaching, developing and recognising their team's achievements so that everyone wins. However, sadly this is not consistently true across the board.

We all know a bad manager, or have experienced a bad manager, though hopefully no one wants to be a bad manager given the choice. The definition of bad ranges from outright unacceptable behaviour to a simple clash in personalities; it is how you experience the manager that will define this for you.

When finding yourself in a situation where your relationship with your manager is strained or less than supportive, and this starts affecting you, it can be daunting. Do you put up with it, report it, run from it, or even bolder, do you try to change the manager? It's important to note that not all bad managers are necessarily doing anything wrong; rather, different management styles and different characters affect people in different ways and some of this can be limiting for individuals.

I try my hardest to be the best manager I can, though I remain open-minded to the fact that I may not be everybody's cup of tea. Understanding how each manager/employee relationship is experienced is a very personal thing, so I hesitate to suggest, concretely, exactly how this should be handled. Everyone is different. However, having seen and experienced a range of situations, I would suggest considering the following steps for handling and surviving a bad manager, and ultimately, moving on from the episode constructively and with learning.

Don't blame yourself

No matter what type of issue you have run into with a 'bad' manager, this is not your fault. You are not and cannot be responsible for how your manager behaves, so don't let anyone hint that that may be the case. I had a situation, many years ago now, where my immediate manager was clearly not very comfortable at work. He was impatient, often angry and clearly frustrated about something. Whether that was due to work or personal circumstances was not the point; the fact was, he brought everything to the table.

One day, he literally threw things at the table – my table, actually – narrowly missing hitting me. To say I was surprised at that moment is an understatement, and in the flash of a second, while it happened, I questioned whether I did something to provoke it and if I should have seen it coming? What I did, in reality, was sit there quite stunned for a few moments, never having experienced physical aggression in the workplace. The work style this manager had was very much about diminishing the contributions of other people and asserting himself, usually as being smarter. I'm all about the practical stuff and getting things done, and there was some element of a character clash.

On reflection, I didn't blame myself, but I did start to pay closer attention to this individual's actions. I shared the incident with a couple of colleagues, and one individual's reaction was: 'What did you do to provoke him?' I replayed in my mind the few sentences which preceded his actions. It came down to my suggesting a course of action different to the one he had suggested during a planning conversation and why I really didn't like what he was forcefully insisting, quite unreasonably, that I do.

Now, regardless of whether my words served as the final straw before the action, there is simply no excuse for being violent in the workplace. Each individual is responsible for their own actions and emotions. It turned out that the manager was known for this behaviour, and yet nothing had been done. I didn't stay long in that role, as you might expect.

Moving not so far away, I learned that he soon reached the end of the road at the company. The shortcomings or frustrations of your manager will never be your responsibility, so do not start taking the blame for their lack of control and putting up with unreasonable actions.

While that example is quite an extreme one, if we strip away the emotional control of the manager it shows a real mismatch in management styles and understanding of what motivates me to deliver my best. I don't respond to diminishment and displays of forced control; I do respond to encouragement and involvement.

I have come across a number of individuals in recent years who have not succeeded in progressing, much to their dissatisfaction. In my role as either manager or mentor, probing to understand what was driving the situation, it emerged that these individuals didn't receive any coaching. In fact, in some situations there was feedback which they needed to hear which was not delivered. Had the feedback and coaching been available, then these individuals would likely have had a very different level of confidence in themselves and a different, more positive, reputation. They had assumed that they didn't deserve to make progress due to their own capabilities when, in my opinion, their previous managers had done a poor job at developing them. Fortunately, this was fixable, and the individuals could learn that it was not their fault. Taking ownership is something which I encourage, but this should not be about accepting blame without question. So, if you find yourself taking responsibility to compensate for a manager, then pause and think how you can shift that mindset.

Understand the challenge

Noticing that the situation with your manager is less than optimal for you may take some uncovering. However, I would hope that not everybody gets objects thrown at their desk before they identify a problem. We've seen that you can identify your needs by reflecting on your current work context, and your experience with your manager will be a rich source of insight here. Are you getting what you need? Are you feeling valued, and is your work recognised? Does your manager communicate with you, and do they create an environment that is supportive? Are you being heard? Are your goals and workload realistic?

All these questions will help identify the source of your dissatisfaction and the start of any tension in the relationship. There are, of course, other elements which have nothing to do with your 'ideal' needs; rather, they are basic expectations, including things like safety and respect. Should there be a problem there, then company reporting policies on harassment and misconduct should be considered. For anything else, trying to identify just why you feel that there is an issue will help you decide whether fixing it is insurmountable or not. If you are unsure, speak to colleagues – starting with those who also report to the same manager. Sometimes, a manager's behaviour may simply be down to their lack of self-awareness, and therefore the whole team could be experiencing what you have. Other times, when it's not widespread, you need to understand why you are feeling frustrated, being treated differently or perceiving that to be the case.

I have had a situation in the past where, through a department restructure (another one, see how common they are!) I found myself working for somebody who evidently had yet to manage more senior people. Having 20 years' experience in managing people at this stage, this was a situation which didn't work well for me. In this case, the situation was not down to the manager expressly trying to treat me differently; rather, their approach was misaligned with my needs and the expectations I had of a manager at that stage.

Sometimes there are just personality clashes too. I have come to terms with the fact that, in life, there are people who attract and people who repel, and interpersonal chemistry does exist.

Some relationships just won't work. Recognising that the issue is down to character or an intangible something is OK. It will be up to you whether you decide to move because of it, but sometimes just recognising that this is the cause might make it easier for you to persevere a little longer under that manager.

Some of the frequent issues I come across via colleagues or people I mentor are managers that just don't do enough for their people. In this situation, the individual has no avenue for development, gets little if any recognition, and communications are poor. Others involve working for micromanagers who simply sit on your every move, dismissing achievements and progress in the hope that individuals try harder as a result. I can't say I've ever been motivated by somebody telling me that I'm rubbish in the hopes that I try harder; it feels like psychological torture to me. It is, however, a style of management I have seen in play.

So, there are many sources of what makes a bad manager for you. The point is that it is your discomfort or disappointment that needs fixing. Taking just a moment to understand the cause will help you in your urgency to resolve the problem or move on.

Have an open conversation

If you have an avenue for open conversations with your manager, then that would be the easiest place to start. Ask if you can have a word or raise it in a regular one-on-one meeting. If you cannot speak to your manager, then speak to your HR representative or a close colleague instead. Giving voice to the issue you're experiencing may help to clear up misunderstandings and correct things quickly. Sometimes, managers are unaware of how their behaviour or their management style is affecting people – in which case, it's usually an easy fix.

Contract together

At the start of all reporting relationships, it is good to exchange how each of you work best and for you to communicate what you need. Sometimes, a revisit is needed. I had an individual in one of my teams, not so long ago, who was slightly more junior than the rest of the team and who desired and benefitted from a very direct and hands-on approach to their work. My style is to give autonomy to my teams, and I extended the same space to this individual. Unfortunately, that was not a desired way of working for him and, being the only one who wanted to work in that way, it created tension within the team. His peers wanted to maintain autonomy for themselves and for him to catch up and adjust. Luckily, the individual brought this to my attention in our face-to-face meeting. I hadn't understood that this would have been such a frustration, though his explanation made it very easy for me to adjust. I was able to explain to other team members the changes and reassure them it wouldn't impact the way the team was working. Very easily, the issue disappeared.

However, had that individual not brought it to my attention, not felt able to let me know what he needed, then we would have all continued promoting this unappealing environment for him, and that would have been detrimental to both him and the team.

Explore with examples

When bringing issues to the manager's attention, particularly when this has to do with their management style, it is helpful to have examples in mind to help highlight how things are experienced and perceived. I had a situation working under a manager who was completely blind to their lack of softer skills, having reached their position through a strong, task-related performance. Being able to see exactly what was missing, I took this issue up directly with that manager. Instead of accusing or pointing out failures, I tried to highlight examples of tactics that I had used in the past which have shown to work. These were simple things like taking steps to improve listening, ensuring no communication gap or prioritising employee and team – in some respects, people-management basics. This proved useful, not only to make the point, but to allow that manager room to fail gracefully and recover all in one.

Not everyone will feel comfortable in doing that, but to keep things neutral and constructive, providing tangible examples looks towards providing solutions rather than blaming people for problems. Managers themselves are all different, and they learn through different means. Some progress into this role of management responsibility via a performance in their individual roles and not because of a talent for management per se.

So, be patient if you can. There is no guarantee that these things will work. However, when faced with the inconvenience of moving teams, you will at least know that you tried everything before giving up on what might otherwise have been a fulfilling role for you.

Business is never personal

A key tenet I have always held to is that business should never be personal. That way, it is possible to have tough conversations without offending anyone. When it oversteps the mark and becomes personal, it is no longer professional and seldom constructive. As you frame your conversations with your manager, keep the focus on your needs, expectations and support, etc., and not about shortcomings in their character, however tempting it may be. When you are feeling wronged or let down, this is less easy to do, so prepare how you want to broach the subject and stick to the evidence and examples.

Seek a neutral sounding board

If you are not able to broach the subject with your manager, or after raising the issue, the situation goes unchanged or deteriorates, find someone to share your experience with. Checking in with teammates is an easy first step if you all share the same challenge with your manager. Often, the way you experience your manager can be positively altered when you hear how others deal with the same individual. It may be that safety in numbers takes the edge off the whole thing, once you realise you are not alone in your thinking. Ask colleagues how they deal with it, and see if you can find a way to work around it. When it is not that simple to ignore, you might need to agree among yourselves whether it is something to be escalated in order to seek help from an alternative manager (or HR). This will give you a first step towards making a change.

Other individuals, further removed from the direct reporting relationship, can often pass feedback to your manager in a way that they are more open to hearing. I have seen this done quite effectively when a manager was very unaware of their lack of listening skills and habit of micromanaging.

Decide on 'pattern' or 'blip'

All managers have off days, and while they should have the emotional intelligence to keep that out of the workplace, they are also only human, and things can spill over from time to time. Recognising whether your feelings around a relationship are driven by a one-off event or a pattern of repeat behaviour will make a difference in how you respond to any issues and how patient you might want to be in solving your situation. Are you being singled out, or is it affecting everybody? How wide is the pattern? Give yourself a window of time to notice if it improves.

Fixing the situation is far easier than moving on, and blips are easy to work through, whereas a pattern will be something that will eventually become too much if left. I pride myself on being an inclusive, personable manager but, yes, I have had my moments, most of them in the sleep-deprived years of new parenthood! I was not my most patient then, and looking back, knowing that my own style became compromised at times, I now strive every day to be extra accommodating. I got the wake-up call that was necessary through feedback, and it makes me a better manager today.

So, consider if someone is having on an off-day and needs patience and the benefit of the doubt or if they need further help. Managers have reputations too.

Don't carry the negative experience to your next role

When you are forced to move on from a position to solve an unworkable manager relationship, it will be normal to feel hard done by, at least for a while. Remember not to talk negatively about that manager in your next role. Not only is it unprofessional to spread negative stories, but the situation may not be like that for everyone – manager/employee relationships differ – and you will likely do yourself damage in the process. Your manager will hopefully learn from the situation, and they may change their ways. Equally, however, they may still be blind to how they affect people and you will only loose energy dwelling on it.

In whatever way you experience and tackle a bad management relationship, you will come out stronger and you will have learnings. I've been most fortunate to have many great managers, and I appreciate that much more as my career progresses. However, from both the positive and negative experiences, I now understand much more acutely what I need, and I seek that out whenever I look for new opportunities. Managers who are highly focused on helping their people succeed are plentiful, so I hope you seek them out too and try to be one.

What does 'good' look like?

When a manager situation is hampering your fulfilment, it is easy to say what we don't like rather than articulating what we need and look for in a manager. There is a lot of truth in the saying 'people don't leave companies, they leave managers', with reasons like lack of appreciation or recognition, communication and trust being high on the list. Yet, surprisingly, this is a piece of the puzzle not considered highly enough at the start point when seeking new roles.

Having worked through the 'work style' section in the product map, along with the needs list from Part 1, it makes sense to define and remind yourself what you need from a manager so that you can build it firmly into your search criteria. If, like many entrepreneurs I have worked alongside, you don't want a manager at all, then listen to what this tells you. Perhaps you are looking for the wrong type of job! In addition to helping you secure the best manager for yourself, reflecting on what makes a bad or good manager can help you to give thought to what type of manager *you* would like to become. If you are already a manager, then this reflection should serve to ensure you 'walk the talk', or help you to identify where focus or improvement could help you become an even better manager. It is shocking to think that about two thirds of managers don't get management training, and so actively owning this early on will help you to identify and model behaviours that are positive.[12]

Armed with full awareness of what you need from a manager and why you may be struggling with the one you have today, this knowledge will stand you in great stead to express your needs and your learnings through the process.

> **Reflection – The manager for you**
> Think of the best manager you have had. What made it
> a positive experience? What about the worst manager?
> What didn't work? Try to express these as needs for
> your search criteria.

Identifying for yourself what works and what doesn't is a great
way to think about the effect you have (or will have one day) on
your direct reports. Extracting the 'best bits' of many managers
you have experienced, combined with your own style, will ensure
you do so in an authentic way.

10

The Coach – Helping Others

UP TO THIS POINT, we have primarily been considering the two mirrors and the cheetah as it applies to you as an individual, to help you understand yourself and your career path. However, the construct can apply equally for you as a manager. Perhaps you already manage people, or hope to do so at some point; if so, then *Two Mirrors and a Cheetah* will help you to develop your people as well as yourself.

The idea that you can't really help other people until you've learnt to help yourself is a common one, and it holds a lot of value in many areas of life. However, it's not strictly true here. You don't have to have applied the model to your own career first before you can use it to help your team. On the contrary, many of you who are already managing people might recognise some of the elements described in this book as things you're already doing when looking after and developing your team members. Looking at this through the eyes of a manager may even help you to explore the framework more easily for yourself.

As a manager and leader, you hold the key to opportunities

and you shape much of the world that people experience at work. You likely have the power to create projects, fund initiatives, assign resources, structure teams, delegate tasks and give responsibility to people. In addition, in the close relationships you forge with your people and teams, you can enable open and honest feedback. You will have a voice that is listened to, which will not only help your team see what is sometimes staring them in the face but also introduce them to new horizons of possibility. There is so much more to management than this book can cover, but here are some key thoughts as to how *Two Mirrors and a Cheetah* can help you in people management.

Help people to understand themselves – mirror one

I often view my role as a manager as one of protector, shielding the team from the 'crap' that cascades down and removing hurdles so that they can focus on delivering and being their best in order to achieve our goals. This sometimes means helping them get out of their own way! Managing individuals, beyond simply getting the work done, is about creating the conditions where people can thrive and be their best selves. When we think back to the steps required to uncover better self-awareness that we looked at earlier in the book, we can see that a manager has a unique role in not only setting the conditions but being a key part of delivering some of the insight. Setting yourself up to be able to do that is critical.

Connect with individuals

To be in the best position to help your team members, you need to create a personal connection. I would argue that this is the first step in any manager/employee relationship, and that prioritising it will help you gain trust and respect. Ensuring you treat each person as an individual requires you to get to know them. For them to be able to treat you as the individual you are requires you letting them get to know you too. It's another two-way street!

My first actions in any new job I've had, certainly over the last 15 years or so, has involved planning an individual conversation with everybody in my immediate team. Where possible, this also includes *their* direct reports too. In any new role, I aim to have these conversations happen within the first 30 days – or the first 60 for particularly large teams. I invite each one to tell me about themselves; what they like, how they made their journey to this point and, critically, what they expect from me in my new role. In return, I share more about myself and seek to build that bond, which hopefully makes me approachable.

Those who have gone through that process with me let me know that not only do they find it hugely valuable, but they have been pleasantly surprised that I care about what they have to say. This is apparently not something that everybody does. You get so much more interaction and genuine input from people when you talk to them individually or in small groups, rather than trying to tackle a new team by simply doing a large Q&A session.

Beyond the initial get-to-know-you conversations, you need to maintain that connection. I frequently walk around my teams or visit them when they're not located in the same spot, and I go and see internal customers together with my team. Being part of the action, as a manager, helps people to really connect with you, rather than remaining in your metaphorical ivory tower, which can increase the distance between you and the teams as well as weakening any relationships you might have. Knowing your people and connecting with them is a commitment, and it requires you to observe. Do this regularly and not just through formal channels of communication. Ironically, those are when your people are least likely to be themselves. Prioritise people in your agenda in order to make it happen!

Feedback

Providing feedback on performance or team working capabilities is a vital way to help individuals have a true perception of themselves. Doing this in a timely and constructive way will help people learn to incorporate it. Helping your team to deal with this feedback openly and positively, and to actually apply it, is a huge enabler. Not all feedback sinks in straight away, and not every individual is able to accept firm but fair messages, so your role in helping translate feedback into actionable improvements will be invaluable. As you observe your team and the various interactions, you will also have insights as to how individuals work in different settings; again, helping people see this will be a powerful aid to their development.

Don't avoid delivering the tough messages; this may hold some of the most valuable learning, even if the individual only works that out much further down the line. Do you check in with your people to ensure that they understand feedback and take steps to digest and action it? When I look at the biggest surprises I faced in receiving what was extremely harsh feedback, it usually came out of nowhere as a thunderbolt. Yet the symptoms were building up over time, though nobody had checked consistently that I was aware of them.

Giving people feedback as a monumental blow, and only at the point where situations escalate, gives the employee a massive mountain to climb in turning the situation around. It is less likely to be successful than giving somebody feedback on a regular basis, and in small digestible amounts, so that they can action it without having an identity crisis.

> **Reflection – Giving feedback**
> Now that you have spent time understanding yourself and the role of feedback for you, what would you do

differently for your team? Can you make changes to improve the feedback they receive from you?

Training

Learning on the job is great. However, well-chosen training does deliver powerful insights. This is, of course, blatantly obvious. However, I have noticed, in more recent times, with the increasing number of start-ups on tight budgets and large companies opting for home-grown courses in scalable formats, face-to-face classroom training is frequently replaced with video-recorded e-learning, which may be less suitable for some topics.

Working with your team to identify the types of training to invest in to create the biggest impact for the individual as well as the organisation is where you, as a manager, can play a role. Shape the development of individuals, not just within their role and your company, but for everything beyond your current company too. Set them up for wherever they go. In doing this, you are investing not only in the skills of the individual but in their motivation and commitment, attributes which can have far greater value as time progresses. Richard Branson captured this sentiment with his now famous quote, first written in 2014: 'Train your staff well enough that they are able to leave, but treat them well enough that they choose to stay.'[13]

Career development conversations and planning

Apart from day-to-day interactions, you also have a role as manager to encourage your teams to think about their development plans, to understand what motivates them and help them develop goals in order to achieve their ambitions. The exercise in Chapter 1 can be used here. Less than half the managers that I have had over my career did this. Sometimes, when I set up processes with new teams, many of them find it surprising, although very welcome, that I choose to do this. This is not happening as far and wide as it could. Not all managers and organisations can deliver on the career plans that are put together, but that's no reason to avoid undertaking it. If you want to draw in high-performing talent, I'd hope you would wish to have a reputation for developing people.

As we looked at in the section on internal moves, many moves are unplanned and opportunities can surface sporadically. In order to move talent effectively on behalf of your organisation, you'll need insight into the desires, career goals and motivators of your team so that you're well placed to highlight where talent can take advantage of unplanned opportunities.

When I look at some of the moves that I am most grateful for, at least one was because of its confidential nature and not something that I could've applied for in the normal way. The opportunity came to me. I was fortunate to have a strong manager who checked in with me as I was returning from my first maternity leave. Knowing me well enough from my past performance, coupled with his understanding of my desire for adventure and a willingness to travel, he put me in the frame for the opportunity. This is not an opportunity I could've sketched out as my next move because the company didn't yet exist within the portfolio. But, ultimately, the career plans I had shared meant a match was still able to be made.

Stretch assignments

Fear stops many people achieving all that they are capable of, and as a manager responsible for the work individuals handle, you have the power to push them at an appropriate pace and let them prove to themselves what they can do. Stretch opportunities, a project or task running parallel to the 'day job', are a great way for you to develop your team in a low-risk way without them having to jump teams. Seeing people achieve more than they thought possible is extremely rewarding, so build it in to your repertoire too. Remember, however, not to penalise those who don't take as well to such opportunities; not everybody will perform in the same way in every role. The goal is to stretch positively, not overburden!

You have the power to help someone see what may be right under their nose; to learn about themselves. Be generous, and use this power graciously.

Build people up – mirror two

Let's go back to the example of the Evil Queen from Snow White. This woman is entirely at the mercy of the words of the mirror. As a leader, whether you see it or not, you have the ability to build up someone's world or bring it crashing down with your choice of words. Do not underestimate the impact you have. It even goes beyond your words. People will watch your actions more than you might think.

When I was working as managing director of a manufacturing and distribution business, with a great deal of employees on site, most days I would walk through the production area and across the bridge into the offices. I carried a small bag containing my high heels. Obviously, for safety reasons, I didn't walk through the production area wearing them, and I drove to the office in my safer flat shoes anyway.

Now, there is nothing particularly special about that, but when I was leaving that business, among the well wishes and in the speeches that followed, one of the employees said: 'We will miss you walking across the bridge with your shoe bag.' It was something so inconsequential – but they were watching me and knew exactly the contents of my bag.

Here's another example. As CEO in Poland, I always got out and about and walked around the factory floor, visiting the warehouses and speaking to people.

One afternoon, two years into my tenure, a lady from the packing lines came up to me and said: 'Your advice on day one is really true, and thank you for keeping your promise.' I had promised to be open and communicate to help change the culture, but honestly, I think that this lady was simply happy that I even spoke to her, given that my predecessor had never done so. She could remember every single thing I said two years later. Coincidentally, I too know exactly what I said, because I had had to write it down in Polish, and the words were among my very first in that language, prepared by me for my introduction.

The point is that even the stuff that you may not think is important, or that you may not think anybody even notices, is being seen and remembered. As the leader, what you say and do *matters*.

Perception is reality

In fact, what you say and do matters so much that your intention – or lack of it – is less important than the perception you create. I remember one particular time when my two boys were very small, and like many parents, I was permanently exhausted. My interpersonal reactions were not to the standard I would have liked, and I accidentally upset someone with how I spoke to them. I can try and explain it to myself as being due to my tiredness, and focusing on a certain important task in that moment when everything was busy but, ultimately, that does not excuse me of responsibility for the way in which my words were received.

So, again, you as leader or manager have the power with your words to change how people feel. It's very important to be mindful about how you act and how you are perceived. Even when words and actions are unintentional, perception *is* reality for the individual experiencing it. As a manager, you could be perceived as overly critical or aggressive if you don't take care about how your words are received.

Recognise the responsibility you have, your visibility and your power to affect people, and use it wisely and with integrity. To keep myself true, I keep the following quote, often attributed to Maya Angelou, in mind: 'People will not remember what you say, they may not remember what you did, but they will never forget how you made them feel.'[14] So, remember to be kind. As a manager and leader, you have a great opportunity to shape conditions and help your people develop and succeed, but always remember that, whether with intention or by lack of attention, you can hamper their progress and block their development.

> **Reflection – How does your team perceive you?**
> Do you know how your team perceives you? Do they think you are helping them to develop? What mechanisms do you have to help you get this insight? Can you create one?

Set the right tone

Your overall style of managing, whether in meetings or other interactions, sets the tone and creates the environment. You can choose to cultivate confidence, encourage contributions and listen, or you can create a hostile confrontational environment that discourages participation. Sadly, with a lack of self-awareness, managers can let situations like the latter take root.

Take the time to listen to, encourage and nurture all individuals and you will be more inclusive and productive. This, in turn, will allow all your increasingly self-aware and unique individuals to bring their diverse perspectives to the discussions you facilitate and the work you all do. Allow feedback to reach you if your style doesn't work for some.

Important, alongside doing the right thing, is standing up

for the right thing too. Your responsibility as a leader does not end with your immediate team. Leverage the gravitas you have and the respect that you command in the position you are in to ensure that any 'bad actors' are rooted out or any behaviour that goes against what you believe is right is called out. Peer feedback is easier to give, so don't limit this to your direct reports alone.

Celebrate successes (even the small ones)

Everyone likes a pat on the back now and then; it's a self-esteem booster. It is just as easy to show appreciation for work done well as for major wins, so be a manager who gives credit where credit is due. Whether it is awards, shout outs, thumbs up, accolades or team events, take time to acknowledge and praise individuals for their work. This creates a positive atmosphere, and everyone will know that their contributions are valued. It signals, too, that you care and are paying attention to what actually gets done. Say 'thank you' and 'well done' as often as you can.

It is easy to get used to people delivering against goals that are set, particularly when you have strong, competitive people in the team, but it is also easy to demotivate without realising it. I worked for one manager who, nice as they were, never said 'well done' more than once over the course of two years, despite my achievements. You can see how that one stuck with me!

Put your own idea of what is needed aside and err on the side of over-celebrating. Involve the team too, so that good work can be admired, learned from and provide a source of inspiration for others.

> **Reflection – The small things that matter**
> Can you recall the last time you said 'thank you' or 'well done'? Could you do it more often?

Help people navigate – the cheetah

We have defined the context of a job as covering the range of needs connected to job, manager and company. Many of these can be shaped by you as a manager, hopefully for the better. Ensure that you understand how your team perceive you so that you are not at risk of being that 'bad' manager. Put your people first and yourself second, and you should avoid that. Your personal approach to working and your style of management will hugely impact the teams of people you have working for you. You know how you work, so let people understand it and take responsibility for the environment and culture you create. Don't just see this as something the company does. Paying attention to the following will help you shape an environment that people not only succeed in, but which will drive your reputation as a manager.

Context + skills = capability

As a manager, you want your team to deliver, so it is important to recognise that their skills alone will not get you there. Teams working in different directions can have great intentions, but they will lose it in the execution. Similarly, you can have brilliant problem solvers, but if they are afraid to speak out and bring the right challenge when it's needed, then those talents will be wasted.

Creating environments where everyone can feel at ease, be themselves and know they have your support and encouragement, is something you can shape from your very first day. You set the tone, so be accessible and lead by example by being yourself and demonstrating what you want to see. Your team will only be strong when you have set the scene such that everyone is focused on working and not on worrying overly about what you think of them. When a context works for people and they have the requisite skills, only then can you truly have a *capability* for the company.

Communicate openly

Communication is fundamental to trusting, constructive and productive environments. Ask yourself: how safe and secure do you feel when you don't know what is going on or how you fit in? Small steps in this area can make a huge difference to engagement. The start of the COVID-19 pandemic at the beginning of 2020 is a perfect example of where communication makes a difference.

What I did with my own teams was to bring them together virtually, every single day, first thing in the morning, for 30 minutes. This was one way to ensure transparency and to offer reassurance. Even on the days where there was no new news to share, having open communication channels gave comfort to many people. Having the ability to give information as well as receive questions or requests builds a really different dynamic in teams – especially when people are isolated from each other and the office environment.

When a great deal of uncertainty is present, as was the case during the early days of the 2020 pandemic, it was so easy to see how many teams and individuals could easily have headed off in completely different directions, most of which would have been unproductive or at least out of alignment.

Bringing people together, sharing honestly and openly, serves to reassure, engage and, ultimately, align people. This goes for regular communication too, not only through times of disruption. When you have a plan or strategy for your team, sharing it helps people see where their efforts fit in. Refine your communication avenues for everyone's benefit.

Be inclusive and seek diversity

An individual's first point of feeling valued lies with you as manager. Representation and diversity policy sits with the company, but the rubber hits the road with the manager. Cultivate the right environment in the way you listen, support and involve people.

Treat your team fairly and, above all, with respect. Demonstrating welcome, inclusion and encouragement for both them and their contributions will help them all feel comfortable. This is the starting point to everyone being their best selves.

> **Reflection – Inclusion**
> How do you know if your team members are feeling included? Do you have a way of verifying this with them?

Encourage risk-taking, celebrate failure

Without taking risks, or learning to accept and learn from failures, your team will not grow. As a manager, it is critical that you play an encouraging role, boosting your team's self-belief and creating an environment where risk-taking is OK and where there is no shame in failure. It should be seen, instead, as a source of powerful learning. Many people stop trying new things due to their fear of failure and valuable input gets lost.

If the company you are in does not have a culture of risk-taking, this does not mean you can't instil it as a learning mechanism. Competitions that encourage and celebrate the bizarre 'outside chance' entries, or those with the biggest learnings rather than the most success, are ways in which you can endorse the practice. Ensuring that people understand what their performance is related to, and when and how to think about failure, will ensure you balance innovation with the need to deliver.

Advocate for curiosity and change

Recognising when people are peaking and no longer challenged, or indeed where they are struggling, and then encouraging them to reshape their environment or trial other ones, can help them learn a great deal as well as position them to keep developing. They are likely in the 'natural progression' quadrant in the needs versus adaptations matrix, and not doing so could mean you risk losing them! Many people are unaware of the richness of opportunities within their current companies and seek to move on elsewhere.

As a strong manager, sharing more about the organisation and connecting people to different projects, people and teams to allow them to widen their horizons, shows real support for the building of self-awareness. Don't worry about losing your team, as you'll only be hanging on to them longer than you should. If you encourage learning and development, you will have people queuing up to work for you.

Facilitate moves

Some people need a gentle nudge to move on, and others want to move before they have fully achieved in their current role. As a manager, you have a role in helping individuals see when their effectiveness has been reached or not. By investing in career conversations with your people, you can help them gauge the right time for a move – internally or externally.

Be a change agent, not the reason for change

As a manager, you are clearly both a cause of change as well as being someone who can guide people through it.

Firstly, understanding what your team need from you, by listening and setting expectations, can ensure a supportive relationship from the outset and allow for mutual feedback. This can avoid any disappointment and blind spots, thus ensuring you recognise how each of your team perceive you. This is, sadly, overlooked by so many managers. I was guilty of this myself, and it can be so destructive that it merits close attention.

Keeping an eye on the pace of learning and the level of mastery of individuals in their roles will allow you to adapt their workload in terms of interest and challenge and ensure your team do not stagnate. Great managers put their people first and ensure their teams can progress, rather than holding them back to deliver their own goals.

> **Reflection – Where are your team on the matrix?**
> Thinking back to the grid of needs and adaptation, do you know where all your direct reports would fit? Is anyone at risk of leaving? Would you know it if they were? Do you have the right relationship and communication channels in place?

Superheroes are not scalable

As a manager, you know you are a very visible example that many people look up to. While it's commendable to demonstrate that you have self-awareness and that you are able to help people, it's also a good idea to keep things as real as possible. Remembering to bring people with you on the journey, being able to explain things in a way that makes sense and not going too fast for people, keeps you connected.

As so many people grapple with how to be more authentic, to let themselves come to work as they are and to achieve the balance in life that works for them, remember not to try to be perfect if you are trying to achieve this for yourself. This is not to encourage you to compromise in any way, but a reminder that the more you succeed, the bigger the boots you leave to be filled by the aspiring individuals who will succeed you.

One thing that has always slightly annoyed me in the press coverage I've had in recent years is the very fact people want to write articles about a woman in business who has children. It still means that this is an exception rather than the rule. If we are truly to have diverse companies in societies, I am not and shouldn't be an exception. I could, at best, be an example of one of the many different ways that you can have a fulfilling career. I will happily be this example until we reach such a point, so long as it inspires others to go for it.

However, I don't want to be painted as a superhero. By definition, that is living outside what is possible or perceived as possible for the average person, and that is the wrong starting point. There is nothing in the examples that I have shared through this book that you can't do yourself. So, be visible, be your best example as a role model, but make it achievable for others to follow in your footsteps. Let your vulnerable side be seen too; it makes you more human.

11

Finding Your Rhythm

ONCE YOU have worked through the concepts within *Two Mirrors and a Cheetah*, you will see how the elements are interlinked and influence each other. Together, these parts can have a big, positive impact on your career. Knowing yourself, being yourself and understanding context is a rhythm, not a one-off exercise. It is about taking control of them and using them continually so that you can steer your career towards a fulfilling set of experiences.

We all interpret things differently, and the pictures you will have created of your own career throughout this book are personal to you. The important thing is to recognise those images and then iterate, update or evolve them as you progress. Changing how you think is the most powerful lesson in this book. Putting it all into practice may still be the 'imaginary' hurdle you face.

Overcome friction

Friction is nature's way of stopping things moving. It takes more energy to *start* something moving than to *keep* something moving, and this is true in life as it is in physics. Overcoming friction at the start of a process in order to launch something might be where the largest effort is needed, and often it's where we focus. However, friction is everywhere, slowing our movement, and anything will gradually stop unless more energy is applied. This is the same for our actions and intentions. Having a plan that gets you started is great, but one that keeps the movement *going* is critical. For your career, removing the initial friction is simply making the conscious decision to start actively managing your professional path. That first burst of effort is simply spent on doing a little reflection to understand where you are at. If you're serious about having a career that works for you, and committed to making some changes, choose the moment to get started as one where you can begin gradually and which will allow you to continue. Whether you take the exercises and questions from the first half of the book together or one by one, put a stake in the ground. Mark the moment when you're going to start paying attention in more detail; to begin to understand about yourself and your conditions for success.

Think about driving. You don't 'unlearn' how to drive, but you may get a little rusty, or be less confident, if you only get in the car once every five years. In the same way, if you approach your career management as a deep dive that happens only when you want to change jobs, the work will be harder and you may feel less confident with it. Instead, make it part of how you look at things every day. As you progress in your career, you will get better at knowing what works for you without having to look at it very systematically. You will develop much more of an internal compass and a gut feel that will help you make decisions along the way. At the end of the day, career fulfilment is about enjoying and succeeding with the work; being yourself, every day, *in the job,* and not just through the big job changes.

If you have changed how you think, which was the initial goal of this book, you will not likely go back to how you saw things before. However, there is still discipline needed to use and embed the principles.

What's the worst thing that can happen?

My favourite question that I use to challenge hesitaters into action is this: what's the worst thing that can happen? If you've got this far in the book, and the idea of building a career that works for you appeals, but you're still unconvinced that it can be low risk, ask yourself this question. In all the moves that I have made, I never thought whether things might be too difficult or not possible. I just went into things looking at 'how' and not 'if'. If the potential outcome isn't such a bad thing, or if it can be reversed, then essentially you have nothing to lose by taking the step, making a change or taking a chance. You can always learn.

I also issue the same challenge when talking of confidence, the lack of which is a reason some people don't get started. It is a very useful way of getting people to push their limitations back. The power that it gives you to be in a position of having nothing to lose and everything to gain is really incredible. It certainly helped me seriously consider many more opportunities than I would've otherwise looked at.

Revisit and defeat the fear factor

If you have identified something that is stopping you from making the commitment to do this, then look at how you could remove it. Just as we explored in Chapter 2, when considering the benefits of dealing with 'fears', if this is what's holding you back, then try to find ways to get comfortable with it. It could be that other life events mean you don't have the focus to explore this right now, and that is also fine, although big life changes may make this the perfect time to look for career or job changes. Perhaps dwell on it and make a commitment to revisit the idea. Give yourself a fixed time to do this though, to ensure you follow through!

What is balance anyway?

Keeping this new approach going will mean integrating your new thinking into your routines and consistently challenging how and why you do things. This dovetails perfectly with the pursuit of the hot potato of work-life balance. As I alluded to earlier in the book, this is of frequent interest to people when it comes to my life; how do I balance being a senior executive and a mum of two small boys?

To start with, I don't like the phrase 'work-life', and I think the idea of balance is the wrong mental image. The phrasing suggests work is not part of your life, and that the non-work stuff is more valuable to you. Perhaps a better way of framing it would be a work/non-work balance, or maybe paid and non-paid time? I don't love any of these to be honest, because they're all quite strict dichotomies. For most of us, work is a necessity, but that shouldn't mean that it can't be enjoyed! Both work and non-work time is made up of the choices we make, and these choices should *all* feed into your personal definition of success.

Personally, the way I manage it is like this: I seek to find work connected to things that I like, and then I prioritise that work as one of many things in my life so that I move towards a fair distribution of time on the work and the non-work, or the paid and the non-paid. The proportion of time I spend on these different priorities, and over what period of time, is my personal definition of balance. I then pay attention by simply reflecting regularly and taking action if things look different to what I was aiming for and, importantly, I ensure my husband and I work as a team for flexibility.

Choose your perspective

Instead of beating yourself up about the odd times when your life may seem off balance, choose a longer timeframe that works for you in which to define the proportions of time you want to spend on the different priorities you have. The smaller your time window, the harder it is to maintain constant balance. If you look at your activities over a day or week, it is far harder to absorb normal fluctuations than it is when measuring over the course of a month, a year or even five years. If you want to spend a disproportionate amount of time on work at some point, perhaps for a promotion or special launch, then do so. Just try to offset that with a disproportionate amount of time later, on other things, in order to readdress the distribution of your time over the longer haul. Remember to reflect on your mental health so that those periods of extra focus do not result in burnout and create issues.

Accept that balance can have motion

Balance is hard to achieve and maintain if you view it as a state of equilibrium that is static – either balanced or not – like a game of Jenga. Here, unbalanced equals collapse! This is not a helpful image as there is little scope for a compensating action.

Think about standing on one foot, even momentarily, something we will all have done at some point. I do it in yoga. (Like many things about yoga, it's a lot harder to master than it sounds!) I don't stand still perfectly, but I try, and I improve over time. As I keep the raised foot off the floor, the muscles in my foot and ankle are tensing back and forth, compensating continually to sustain the pose. Why not have a go now? Stand up and raise one foot. I would imagine most of you are wobbling back and forth but probably succeeding in keeping the foot off the floor? You might feel the same sensation in your foot as I do, or if you were a little less steady, you may have used your arms to help compensate for your unsteadiness. Either way, you are balancing on one foot! Now, focus on something in front of you. This makes it easier to control the wobbling. It gives you a reference point and provides another compensating force. Once you have managed a balance, try closing your eyes. Chances are you will fall off balance far sooner. Our minds need the sight reference as a part of the process of compensating, as it helps us calculate how to regulate the opposing movements.

Now, let's take the same principles into our idea of work-life balance. What may look static actually involves an abundance of small, constant adjustments and continued effort and attention. A static split between 'work' and 'life', with a clear and clean separation, is *never* going to be sustainable. The art of balance is about accepting movement but being in control of the variations, avoiding the extremes that lead to collapse. The perfect work-life equation is an integration; a rhythm. To succeed is to have mechanisms that allow you to see when you approach the extremes and to be able to compensate using your self-awareness to maintain your centre of gravity – that ability to be you!

Practice makes better

The more you practise the ideas behind *Two Mirrors and a Cheetah*, the more it will become second nature, and you will find your own rhythm. Seek to improve but not to be perfect – don't slip back into the idea that there is an ideal you need to force yourself to live up to. After all, this is a book about dropping that exact fixation! My youngest son has a phrase that I find easier to adopt. Every time he couldn't do something, be that clicking his fingers or doing a hula hoop, I encouraged him to keep trying by saying 'practice makes...'. Instead of saying the word 'perfect', he would always answer 'better'. That works so well as a simple vision of continuous improvement – practice makes better!

The key to sustaining anything that involves a change in habit is to make it gradual. As you learn and explore new approaches, not everything will be right straight away. Particularly as you find ways to change behaviour and 'be yourself', it is completely normal to trial things, and in doing so, you will find new ways of doing things that work for you. You will push your level of comfort, and only you can know when you push it too far. Test things to find what works, learn where your limits are and choose manageable changes that you can land firmly and easily repeat with ongoing success.

Learn to break eggs

This concept is something I use to encourage my teams to be bold about time management. In learning to prioritise the big things among the non-stop flow of inbox tasks, some things will be missed. You must get comfortable with that. Particularly as you begin to 'be yourself' and prioritise according to your values, it is easy to see that part of practising will be getting it wrong – missing something important perhaps. Don't worry. Rather than stalling because you worry about juggling priorities and dropping something important, potentially creating a mess, try to shift your focus. If you accept that you will drop a metaphorical egg or two from time to time, you can move on from fear to simply focusing on cleaning them up faster! It's like the automation example again, but applied to your personal planning process. The more you try not to do something, the more you might find that you do it – simply because you are focused on avoiding it.

So, as you keep practising, smash those eggs and improve how fast you clean up!

Momentum for everyone

As you succeed at being yourself, driving your own career and gaining fulfilment, you are contributing to a greater goal. What better thought to help sustain your own momentum? It might be counterintuitive to think that focusing so acutely on yourself can be something that will drive benefits for many others, but it can. In recent years, I've been passionate about driving better diversity and inclusion in organisations, whether that's gender, sexual orientation, religion, ethnicity, disability or age. As many others do, I believe that having a more equitable society and place to work is a first step in creating a truly inclusive environment. This is what all societies, communities and businesses need in order to see better results. At the heart of encouraging diversity is getting everybody to turn up to work or in their daily lives *as themselves*; to take off the mask and to stop acting because they can now feel comfortable with who they are and where they are. By encouraging everybody to have greater self-awareness, we can have more people coming to the table understanding what unique powers, skills and perspectives they have. This is a *vital* first step.

Then, assuming we have that understanding in abundance, the next step is making sure those individuals can hold on to what, who and how they want to be without feeling that they have to revert back to hiding behind a 'mask'. It means helping people to feel accepted and that they fit in; helping them to walk the tightrope of compromise without hiding their unique qualities.

Mirror number two stands for everything we need to do in businesses to ensure that we don't kill the diversity that we already have. The role of the managers and leaders is not only to support people to believe in themselves, but nurturing and cultivating environments that are inclusive.

I've often heard the quote: 'If diversity is being invited to the ball, then inclusion is being asked to dance.' I love this, but I'd also like to push the metaphor further. Maybe true inclusion is not being *asked* to dance. Maybe true inclusion does not have the power dynamic of an inviter and an invitee, but instead it's a ball where everybody feels *free* to get up and dance when they want and how they want – just one big dance party!

If we look at where we are today, we undoubtedly need to make changes across many organisations to better achieve representation. This means that many people will need to move roles and enter new industries to allow a balance in representation to be achieved and maintained. Whether people move driven by initiatives or by newfound confidence and displays of authenticity is not the issue. In order to have all those movements happen within organisations, cultures and geographies, we need to collectively recognise the difficulty of moving.

It requires us to equip individuals and organisations to deal with and encourage movement. So, the cheetah is very much something for everybody to think about in terms of mobilising and preparing for the momentum that we all need to see in order to gain collective balance.

Start moving yourself when it fits. Share how to move, and encourage others to embrace movement.

Closing reflection

I started this book with a challenge to you to describe yourself as a piece of pasta. My hope, now that you have reached the end, is that you can not only tell me which piece of pasta you are, but also the ideal cooking instructions, accompanying sauce and even the wine that will ensure your pasta is appreciated at its best!

I hope you have enjoyed the stories I've told, learned a little about yourself and found the process to be helpful for your career or, indeed, in your life beyond. If so, perhaps pass the advice from this book along to inspire someone else. If you no longer need it, you could even give the book to someone else – that way it doesn't sit on the shelf collecting dust! Good luck in making the choices and changes you want and gaining greater fulfilment in your career as a result, as *yourself*.

My final thought is to leave you with the answer to perhaps the most overused yet helpful question I have come across in the many years of attending or speaking on panels.

What advice would I give to my younger self?

Quite simply, I would say, 'Slow down a little, and perhaps don't try so hard. Things will happen, but it's patience that helps you see how. Everything is possible, it is just a question of what trade-offs you need to make. Remember: it is not all about you, so be kind. But you should also be bold, go for it and do it with conviction. Above all, enjoy.'

Acknowledgements

The inspiration for this book came via a keynote speech I gave in Munich, on International Women's Day in 2017, when the theme was: 'Be Bold for Change'. I gave my speech the title 'Two Mirrors and a Cheetah: Being Bold is Being You.' The stories within that speech were what people found most memorable, along with its random name. I think this was the reason an unusually large amount of people came, and so it stuck.

I have since run personal development sessions using the same framework as I continue to coach and mentor people. As our world of work changes rapidly, I see how people are faced not only with many new career challenges, but specifically with those that an age of authenticity and a drive for better diversity bring, as we all grapple with how to bring our 'whole selves' to work. Passionate about supporting these changes and helping others to navigate them, I decided to develop the session into a book so it could have a wider impact.

My thanks go to all of my colleagues who responded so well to my initial storytelling efforts, and to those who have taken part in the career development sessions. Your feedback and encouragement gave me the momentum to write this book.

Thanks also to all the friends, family and colleagues, past and present, who have helped me in different ways to get this book out. Pausing my full-time employment to write this book was a luxury in learning in so many ways, yet a particularly isolating experience given it coincided with so many months of lockdown during the 2020 pandemic. I missed the energy I normally derive from my work, but all the support I received helped me keep it up. A special mention goes to Tracy Doyle, Kelley Rowe, Ruwan Kodikara, Sebastian O'Keefe and Lauren Monk, who persevered with the earliest version of the book and whose very honest feedback helped me carve out the story that lay among the very rambling text. It was a humbling experience, and your enthusiasm brightened the tougher days in the editing process. Thank you.

I would like to thank my editor, Rebecca Bush, who helped get my work to a much better place. I am grateful for the way you helped me sharpen my focus on the reader. To Sarah Busby and Andrew Dawson, who helped me battle the finer, oh so necessary 'small' details, to build quality into my work. Thanks too to Wayne Kehoe and George Stevens, who helped me craft the manuscript into an actual book complete with personality. Thank you; I love what you did.

My unending thanks have to go to my husband, Riemer, who bore the brunt of the ups and downs of this writing process with me as a first-time author. He genuinely had little escape from my 'thinking out loud' as I brainstormed my way through multiple revisions during lockdown. Your support with our boys lets me continue with amazing flexibility, in a career that energises me, and I am so very grateful to you for that and for everything you do for us.

Note from the Author

Hello, I'm Fiona McDonnell. You will have picked up much of my career from the examples sprinkled through the book. But, to complete the picture, here is a little background to add some colour to those stories.

I grew up in Newcastle, in the north east of England. Both of my parents were teachers, as were two of my grandparents, and business was not something I was exposed to. My grandad, on my father's side, worked at Vicker's shipyard, and when I showed an interest in technical drawing at school, he gave me his draughtsman's compass and instruments. I used them with much pride myself later on. I studied physics, maths and further maths alongside German at college. Not a common combination but perhaps the start of me coming into my own and treading my own path.

I gained a place at Cambridge to study manufacturing engineering and landed a sponsorship with a construction company to part fund it, which meant many holidays spent working on building sites. That opportunity came about after spending one week of work experience there during school. I took a year out prior to university, spending a few months washing dishes and making beds in a hotel in the German Alps, and the rest relining some of Manchester's oldest sewers as the first female site engineer at Kennedy Construction Ltd. I won a bursary award for practical engineering skills from Newnham College, Cambridge, for that too.

Following university, I was attracted to manufacturing and consumer goods as the world of household brands was easy to relate to. My first graduate job was in Munich as my love of adventure took over, and my newfound German came in handy. Becoming a consumer retail director at Amazon, which took me back to Germany many years later, still seems an amazing coincidence, as my route meandered somewhat as you will have noticed.

The 30 years of industry experience that join those two together have taken me through leading organisations from Kraft Jacobs Suchard, Kellogg's, PwC, Nike, Forrester Research, Silvo B.V., Kamis, McCormick & Company and then Amazon. Each step in the earlier days tackled a different function: process development, product management, trade marketing, finance, marketing, strategy, sales and channel management, all of which gave me the toolkit and breadth for general management. From Germany, France, Singapore, the Netherlands, Poland and a couple of UK stints, each role gave me a new cultural experience and often a new language (I picked up three). That kept my learning at the max and my boredom threshold at bay. I supplemented my commercial skills along the way with an MBA in general management from INSEAD and an executive programme from Wharton.

From my first managing director role in the Netherlands for Silvo B.V. to the leadership roles I do today, as the scope and complexity have grown, I continue to enjoy a challenge, and I'm still learning as a leader, finding additional ways to develop, motivate and, hopefully, inspire others. In recent years, I have taken more active roles in promoting diversity and STEM careers, speaking regularly at careers events, facilitating and speaking at industry forums, writing in the media and teaching as a volunteer in schools. In 2018, I took on the role of executive sponsor for diversity at Amazon UK and was the chair of the Women in Innovation Committee, also becoming a public spokesperson for Amazon. I was humbled to be voted Diversity Leader of the Year at the 2019 Tech Leaders Awards.

Alongside the 'day job', I am a board advisor for DIAL Global (Diverse and Inclusive Aspirational Leaders), a teaching volunteer at Working Options in Education and a STEM ambassador. Education, though not the only route for sure, did help me, and I was very much in the minority as both a woman in engineering and in business, so these are natural causes for me to support, and I am both learning and giving back.

What I love about my roles today – whether it's general manager, CEO or director, the title is not as important – is the mix of solving problems, helping people and making things happen. The richness of balancing the internal focus with external stakeholders, be that customers, vendors, media or indeed institutions, gives me the variety, and the inspiration of working with people keeps me engaged. If I am to put a title on it, I would say I am a strategist-catalyst-coach.

When I was growing up, I had a vague idea of becoming a chef, and then later, a stand-up comedian. I did work in many food companies and haven't lost the desire to crack jokes or entertain, though I do it on a different stage!

My passion for culture and travel is still alive, and though I live in Buckinghamshire today with my husband and two boys, who knows what new journeys lie ahead.

Fiona

For more information, or if you want to tell me what you thought of this book, please visit my website at www.fionamcdonnell.com

Please do leave a review wherever you purchased the book, as this will help future readers. Thank you in advance.

Additional Resources

Self-awareness

1. *What Color Is Your Parachute?* by Richard N Bolles

2. *Personal Branding for Dummies* by Susan Chritton

3. *Brand You* by John Purkiss and David Royston-Lee

4. The Myers & Briggs Foundation: https://www.myersbriggs.org

5. A free personality test based on the Myers-Briggs types: https://www.16personalities.com/free-personality-test

6. The nine Belbin Team Roles: https://www.belbin.com

7. Insights Discovery psychometric tool, using the four-colour model: https://www.insights.com/products/insights-discovery/

Getting comfortable with change

1. *Who Moved My Cheese?* by Dr Spencer Johnson

Must reads for managers

1. *Harvard Business Review* article 'Connect, Then Lead' by Amy J.C. Cuddy, Matthew Kohut and John Neffinger, Summer 2013: https://hbr.org/2013/07/connect-then-lead

2. *Good to Great* by Jim Collins

3. *How to Win Friends and Influence People in the Digital Age* by Dale Carnegie & Associates

Additional Visualisation Exercises

If you found the visualisation exercise on goals from Chapter 1 helpful, this section contains two more.

1. **Values**

2. **Team Roles**

EXERCISE 1 – IDENTIFYING LIFE VALUES

Introduction: There are plenty of exercises that get you to imagine your own funeral, whether that is as fly on the wall or a guest at the wake. The concept of giving form to what you would like people to say about you and being concrete about what you want to be remembered for can help you more accurately describe and identify values. It can also be an indication of whether you are indeed succeeding in spending time on the things that you say matter to you.

The Scene: Look out into the future, many years from now, and try to conjure an image in your head of your own funeral. Your nearest and dearest have gathered to give you a 'send off'; to share their grief and loss at your passing and to celebrate your life. You can see the ceremony, view the guests and hear the words that are spoken. As the service progresses, mention is made of the family that survive you and the close loved ones that

will miss your ongoing presence. Stories shared recount
the fun, the very touching and the typically 'you' things
that you did. There is great sadness, yet there is gratitude
for your time in this world.

Later that day, your loved ones are continuing to talk at
the wake and the mood becomes less sombre. The stories
continue, happy memories come out and the guests look
towards their own futures too, citing: 'That's what you
would've wanted.'

Close your eyes and feel it continue for a few min-
utes longer before reading on.

Can you capture the feelings this stirred in you? Who do
you see, and what type of service or wake was it? What
were you remembered for? Were there things that you
did that people were grateful for? How did they describe
you as a character, and what will they miss? Try to be
honest as you build this picture.

Now, bring yourself back to the present day. To draw out
your values, ask of yourself the following four questions:

- How did people describe the way in which you lived?
- What will people miss the most?
- What do you think you will be remembered for?
- Who were the guests?

From those answers, can you identify values for yourself?
Think about what you saw as important.
Being able to describe yourself through the eyes of other
people is an easier way to uncover things like values or,

indeed, behaviours. In the exercise, you are challenged to see the future as an extension of now, and not necessarily to picture it as you would like. It specifically does not ask you to create an ideal scenario. In order to check whether you are prioritising the things you feel are really important and surrounding yourself with the people that support you, ask yourself the following:

- If you managed to picture what you *would like* people to say about you, was that the same as what you *think* they will say about you?
- Any difference in these two scenarios will identify whether or not you are prioritising what you think is important and nurturing your values in practice. If you are not, then this is a valuable wake-up call to reevaluate your path.

Does it reflect the person you want to be?
Does it reflect the things you want to do?

You have the power today to influence the outcome!

EXERCISE 2 – RECOGNISING TEAM OR COMPANY FIT

Introduction: When searching for a new job, either internally or externally, the element of team 'fit' is not really articulated in the job description or visible through the interview process. As with the less tangible things in life, being able to recognise how something makes us feel can help. This team exercise will help you with your 'barometer'.

The scene: Close your eyes and look back to the best job you have had in your career, or indeed a great team you have been part of. You are in a great role that fits everything you love to do. You have brilliant teammates, everyone is helpful, you get on well and it is a stimulating environment. Your manager is great too. They just 'get' you. There is support from all angles and you are able to be yourself, to achieve and really enjoy it.

As you recall the many interactions you experienced, you have a warm feeling. Perhaps it brings on a smile, certainly a feeling of relaxation and contentment. Can you see it? Can you feel it?

Try to dwell on the image and the feeling for as long as you can.

Picture the team and the manager relationship: can you articulate what elements made it so good?

- What was your role, relative to others?
- What type of interactions did you have?
- How did your manager treat and interact with you?
- What made you feel included?

Note what the answers are and if these reflect important needs for you which you can add to your list.

As you look for new companies, roles and teams, recognise the feeling you have as you talk to people there and, importantly, the feeling you have when you first engage with the hiring manager.

Does it make you feel the same way? If so, perhaps this is a good 'fit' for you.

Endnotes

1. Matthew Tull, 'A Basic Guide to Panic Attacks', Verywellmind, February 20, 2021, https://www.verywellmind.com/panic-attacks-2797316

2. Mental Health Foundation, 'Mental Health Statistics: people seeking help', accessed on July 5th, 2021, https://www.mentalhealth.org.uk/statistics/mental-health-statistics-people-seeking-help

3. According to his editor at the *Kansas City Star*, Walt Disney 'lacked imagination and had no good ideas'. Cheryl Welsh, 'Irony of Life: Walt Disney Was Fired From A Newspaper Because Of Lack Of Creativity', March 5th, 2018, https://fabiosa.com/rsako-auemm-pbdmt-phkan-irony-of-life-walt-disney-was-fired-from-a-newspaper-because-of-lack-of-creativity/

4. Li Yiyun, *The Guardian*, Family and Relationships, March 2nd, 2005, https://www.theguardian.com/lifeandstyle/2005/mar/02/familyandrelationships.features11

5. There are multiple theories about how many paintings Van Gogh actually sold during his lifetime. The Van Gogh Museum in Amsterdam suggested he traded paintings for food. (The Van Gogh Museum 2021) The Van Gogh Museum, 'How Many Paintings Did Vincent Sell During His Lifetime?', accessed on July 9th, 2021, https://www.vangoghmuseum.nl/en/art-and-stories/vincent-van-gogh-faq/how-many-paintings-did-vincent-sell-during-his-lifetime

6. 2019 research study by 'My Confidence Matters'.https://www.myconfidencematters.com/research-2019

7. The quote, 'Whether you think you can or you can't, you are right', has been captured in a number of variations and attributed to Henry Ford, Virgil, John Dryden and Mary Kay Ash, among others. Quote Investigator, 'Whether You Believe You Can Do a Thing or Not You Are Right', February 3rd, 2015, https://quoteinvestigator.com/2015/02/03/you-can/

8. Covey, Stephen R. *The 7 Habits of Highly Effective People: Powerful Lessons in Personal Change*. 25th anniversary edition. New York: Simon & Schuster, 2004

9. LinkedIn and Lou Adler, 'How Source of Hire Impacts Job Satisfaction', February 29th, 2016, accessed on July 9th, 2021 https://www.linkedin.com/pulse/new-survey-reveals-85-all-jobs-filled-via-networking-lou-adler/

10. Roy Maurer 23rd June, 2017, 'Employee Referrals Remain Top Source for Hires' (shrm.org), https://www.shrm.org/ResourcesAndTools/hr-topics/talent-acquisition/pages/employee-referrals-remains-top-source-hires.aspx

11. 2017 Millennial Hiring Trends Study MRI Network, https://mrinetwork.com/media/303995/2017millennialhiringtrendsstudy.pdf

12. David Stuart and Todd Nordstrom, March 8th 2018, Forbes.com '10 Shocking Workplace Stats You Need To Know', https://www.forbes.com/sites/davidsturt/2018/03/08/10-shocking-workplace-stats-you-need-to-know

13. Richard Branson, 2014, Quotefancy.com, accessed July 21st, 2021 https://quotefancy.com/quote/285423/Richard-Branson-Train-people-well-enough-so-they-can-leave-treat-them-well-enough-so-they

14. The statement, 'They may forget what you said, but they will never forget how you made them feel', has been attributed to multiple authors, including but not limited to Maya Angelou. Quote Investigator, April 6th, 2014, http://quoteinvestigator.com/2014/04/06/they-feel/

CPSIA information can be obtained
at www.ICGtesting.com
Printed in the USA
LVHW022125230921
698581LV00001B/153